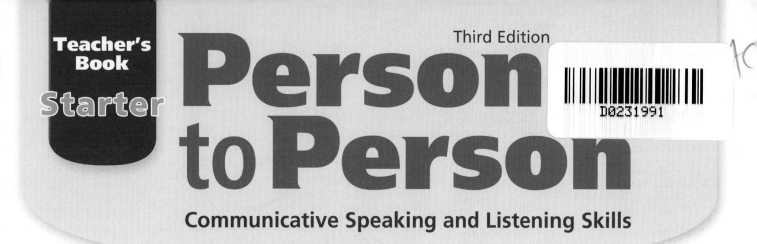

Teacher's Book

Starter

Third Edition

Person to Person

Communicative Speaking and Listening Skills

Jack C. Richards   **Genevieve Kocienda**

OXFORD
UNIVERSITY PRESS

198 Madison Avenue
New York, NY 10016 USA

Great Clarendon Street, Oxford OX2 6DP UK

Oxford University Press is a department of the University of Oxford.
It furthers the University's objective of excellence in research, scholarship,
and education by publishing worldwide in

Oxford New York

Auckland Cape Town Dar es Salaam Hong Kong Karachi
Kuala Lumpur Madrid Melbourne Mexico City Nairobi
New Delhi Shanghai Taipei Toronto

With offices in

Argentina Austria Brazil Chile Czech Republic France Greece
Guatemala Hungary Italy Japan Poland Portugal Singapore
South Korea Switzerland Thailand Turkey Ukraine Vietnam

OXFORD and OXFORD ENGLISH are registered trademarks of
Oxford University Press

Executive Publisher: Nancy Leonhardt
Senior Acquisitions Editor: Chris Balderston
Senior Editor: Patricia O'Neill
Associate Editor: Amy E. Hawley
Assistant Editor: Hannah Ryu
Art Director: Maj-Britt Hagsted
Layout Artist: Elsa Varela
Art Editor: Robin Fadool
Production Manager: Shanta Persaud
Production Controller: Robin Roberson

ISBN-13: 978 0 19 430218 0
ISBN-10: 0 19 430218 0

Printed in Hong Kong.

Printing (last digit): 10 9 8 7 6 5 4 3 2 1

ACKNOWLEDGMENTS
Optional Activities written by Michelle Johnstone
Illustrations and realia by: Geo Parkin: 117, 120, 121, 130; Karen Minot: 126, 133.

Scope and Sequence

Unit 5

Functions	Topics	Structures	Pronunciation Focus
Telling the time, talking about routines, talking about the week, talking about activities	Time, daily schedules, everyday activities	*What time is it?* *Wh-* questions	Stress in questions

Unit 6

Functions	Topics	Structures	Pronunciation Focus
Talking and giving an opinion about school, talking about and comparing personal qualities	Classes, studies, personal qualities	*How* and *what* questions	Syllable stress

Review: Units 4–6

Unit 7

Functions	Topics	Structures	Pronunciation Focus
Talking about routines, asking about the weekend, talking about past events	Weekend activities, past events	*Do you ever…?* adverbs of time, past tense	Pronunciation of *was*

Unit 8

Functions	Topics	Structures	Pronunciation Focus
Asking about meals, asking about likes, asking about wants and preferences	Food and beverages, meals	Asking for something formally, *How about…?* *Do you like…?* *Wh-* questions	Intonation of questions

Unit 9

Functions	Topics	Structures	Pronunciation Focus
Describing qualities, asking about abilities and talents, describing abilities	Hobbies, personal qualities	Adjectives, *Are you…?* *Can you…? What…?*	Pronunciation of *can* and *can't*

Introduction

New to this edition

Student CD

A Student CD is included in the back of the Student Book to provide students with listening practice outside of class.

Consider This

Each unit opens with a Consider This activity. It provides cross-cultural input and serves as a quick introduction to the unit.

Use These Words

This new feature provides vocabulary support for students as they complete the Practice activities.

Now Try This

This addition to the Person to Person pages offers extension activities that can be done as a class or by students who finish earlier than their classmates.

Test Booklet

The completely revised test program now provides photocopiable tests for all 12 units of the Student Book to assess both listening and speaking. There is an audio CD in the back of the booklet containing the listening material. Answer keys and the audio script are also included.

Components

Person to Person, Third Edition, Starter Book consists of:

• Student Book with CD

The Student Book contains 12 units, each unit made up of two lessons. Each lesson contains: a Conversation, Give It a Try, and Listen to This. The Let's Talk activity in the first lesson allows students to practice the functions of the lesson in a less controlled activity. Each unit ends with Person to Person, which gives students an opportunity to work together on task-based communicative activities using the functions taught in the unit. The types of practice range from controlled to free use of the language. Review units after every third unit also consolidate the functions from those units. The Student CD in the back of the book contains Conversations 1 and 2 from each lesson, and can be used by students outside of class for additional listening practice.

• Audio CDs

Person to Person, Third Edition, provides many opportunities to listen to native and non-native speakers. The Class CDs have recordings for:

1. *Conversation.* The conversation that opens each lesson in the unit is presented at a normal, natural speed. Accompanying comprehension questions and answers are provided in the Teacher's Book.

2. *Give It a Try.* Sample dialogue based on the text presented in the function boxes are now recorded to provide students with more listening examples.

3. *Listen to This.* This listening selection includes conversations that will help students perform real-life listening tasks such as finding out about opening and closing times, getting directions, and listening to and writing down information on forms.

4. *Pronunciation Focus.* The examples in the Pronunciation Focus are now included on the CD to further enhance pronunciation practice.

The audio script is at the back of the Student Book. It should not be referred to unless necessary after students have heard a recording several times.

Recorded material is identified by this icon , which includes the audio track number for easy reference.

• Teacher's Book

The Teacher's Book presents step-by-step procedures for teaching each unit. Notes on language, culture, and pronunciation are provided throughout in anticipation of areas that may cause difficulty for students. Optional Activities, which may be photocopied for students, are also provided for each unit. The entire audio script of the Student Book is included in the Teacher's Book.

• Test Booklet

The test package has been completely revised for the third edition. The Test Booklet contains photocopiable tests for each unit in the Student Book, as well as an answer key and audio script. The audio CD in the back of the booklet contains recordings for all of the listening sections of the tests.

A Communicative Approach

Over the years, there has been a de-emphasis on grammatical competence as the primary goal of language learning and a focus on communicative objectives instead. This has resulted in less attention to the rules of English grammar and grammatical accuracy, and more interest in the processes of communication and conversational fluency as a goal in conversation classes. For this reason, the focus of each unit in *Person to Person* is not on grammar, but on conversational tasks or functions, such as talking about likes and dislikes, or asking permission.

Although grammatical competence is a component of conversational proficiency, there are additional skills specific to conversation. Some of the most important of these skills and abilities are discussed below.

Topics

To be able to converse, the learner must be familiar with a broad range of common topics that occur in everyday conversation. He or she needs to be able to respond to and initiate questions on the situations, events, and activities that are commonly referred to during social interaction with speakers of English. This means having sufficient vocabulary not only to be able to recognize what was said, but also to have something to say or add in response.

Speech Functions

When people meet they do more than exchange information. They use language to make social interaction possible. This involves the ability to carry out different kinds of conversational tasks and speech functions, such as to greet and acknowledge people, to open and close conversations comfortably, and to introduce and develop topics naturally. When we speak to people we not only *say* things, we *do* things: we describe events and feelings, make requests, and offer suggestions and recommendations, as well as respond and react to suggestions, requests, orders, and so on. These are the speech functions we use for conversation and which learners of English need to practice.

To illustrate the importance of language functions, let's take the example *will*. In grammar classes students learn that *will* has future meaning. However, *will* covers a variety of functions: prediction (*I think it will rain tomorrow.*), warning (*Be careful or you'll fall.*), offer (*I'll do it.*), request (*Will you open the door?*), threat (*Do that again and I'll scream!*), and promise (*I'll take you out for dinner if you pass the test.*). If students aren't aware of these uses of *will*, they are likely to think that *will* is interchangeable with other future forms, resulting in inappropriate utterances. For example, they need to understand that *Are you going to open the door?* is not equivalent to *Will you open the door?* And the answer to *What are you doing after work?* cannot be *I'll go home.*

Just as a single structure can be used to express a number of functions, so can a given function be communicated by a range of grammatical forms. Consider how many ways advice can be given. We can use modals (*Maybe you should/ought to lie down.*), questions (*Why don't you lie down?* or *Have you thought about lying down?*), or the conditional (*If I were you, I would lie down.*). In order to develop the necessary conversational and listening skills, extensive practice is needed, and this is what *Person to Person* provides.

Unpredictable Forms

When we perform different kinds of speech functions, we usually take part in a series of exchanges. For example, I *invite* you to a movie. You *accept* the invitation and *inquire* where and when we will meet. I *suggest* a time and a place. You *accept* my suggestion or *suggest* an alternative. But although this sequence of functions can be predicted once the function of the first utterance in the series is determined, the *actual words and phrases used* to express each function cannot be predicted. Conversational competence requires the listener to match and understand the meanings of different sentences and phrases according to where they occur within an exchange.

Appropriate Language

The degree of social distance between speakers influences the forms of address used, what is talked about, and how it is said. For each interaction, a speaker must decide what the relationship between the speaker and hearer is, then adjust his/her conversational choices accordingly. Thus, in speaking to a professor a student may ask, *Could I possibly speak with you for a minute?* and to a friend, *Hey, Bob, got a minute?*

As well as using language that is sufficiently polite or casual for the situation, we must also express speech functions according to the conventions of English. We can greet a person in English with *How are you?*, but although the expressions *Are you well?* and *How is your health?* are both English, they are not customarily used as greetings. A great deal of conversational language is, in this sense, idiomatic and conventional.

Mutually Created

Conversation is a two-way process. Participants share the responsibility of maintaining the flow of talk and making their contributions both comprehensible and relevant. Conversational competence thus involves the integration of grammatical skills with the other skills noted above, and practice in this is what *Person to Person* provides.

The functions and topics included in *Person to Person* are based on a consideration of communicative needs and related grammar skills required of students at the basic and intermediate levels. A complete list of the functions and topics appears in the Scope and Sequence on pages iii–v.

How a Lesson Works

Consider This

The first page of each unit contains a Consider This section. These contain factual information related to the topic of the unit. They can be used as a warm-up to the unit, and are intended to introduce cross-cultural information into the lesson.

Time: approximately 5 minutes

Conversation

Each unit has two lessons. Each lesson begins with a recorded conversation that includes examples of the functions to be studied in that lesson. Two subsections—Prelistening Questions and Vocabulary—can help prepare students to listen to the conversation.

Vocabulary

The Teacher's Book suggests vocabulary items for presentation with each conversation. It is up to you to choose if and when to introduce them. You may wish to postpone the introduction of new vocabulary until after the students have heard the conversation once. This will encourage them to get the message from the whole conversation, rather than listen for individual words. Thus, students learn to keep listening even if they hear a word or two they don't understand.

When appropriate, provide a picture or example of the item being introduced. Alternatively, write the word on the board and present the definition given in the Teacher's Book. If time permits, ask students to make an original sentence with each new item. You may also wish to simply translate the word or expression, or allow the students to use a bilingual dictionary. In most instances, students will benefit more from using the context to understand the meaning.

Prelistening Questions

These questions are designed to stimulate students' interest and focus them on the topic of the conversation. Discussing the questions either in pairs, small groups, or as a class enables students to better make use of their knowledge of the topic as they listen to the conversation.

Listening

Students should have several opportunities to hear the conversation. First, play the entire conversation without stopping. Then, play it again with frequent pauses during which students can repeat the lines. They will also read it afterward. As they do so, have them practice the "read and look up" technique:

One student looks at the text to be read aloud. When ready to speak, he or she looks at his or her partner and says a line (or part of a line). He or she then looks down at the page again for the next line, and again looks up while saying it. The reader's eyes should never be in the book while he or she is speaking. This will help students to role-play more naturally. At the same time, it will improve their reading fluency by requiring them to take in phrases, rather than read word-by-word. Although students may resist this technique in the beginning, repeated practice will help them see how useful it is.

Time: approximately 20 minutes

Give It a Try

Every function heard in the conversation is presented separately in the Give It a Try section. This allows each function to be concentrated on individually. Follow the suggestions in the Teacher's Book for teaching pronunciation points where applicable. Notes on culture, grammar, and usage are also provided to enable you to present the functions more effectively. The guided Practice activities give each learner an opportunity to practice the new functions with a partner or in a small group. They include practice with content in the Student Book and provide opportunities for students to use the same functions to practice talking about their own ideas and experiences.

Time: approximately 15 minutes for each numbered
subsection

Use These Words

The "Use These Words" feature is new in this third edition. It occurs once per lesson in the Give It a Try sections, and provides vocabulary support by giving students access to words they can use to do the Practice activities. You can draw students' attention to this as you see fit. As an extension activity, ask students to add to the list by thinking of their own ideas or using their dictionaries for help.

Listen to This

Both lessons in each unit have a task-based listening section called Listen to This, which is designed to help students with real-life listening tasks. Following a presentation of the recording, students listen again to check their own answers before comparing with partners or with the class. Each Listen to This section in the Teacher's Book contains the audioscript and an answer key along with a suggested teaching procedure for that section.

Time: approximately 20 minutes

Let's Talk

Each unit has a speaking activity, Let's Talk, which is presented at the end of the first lesson. It provides an opportunity to practice the functions and vocabulary of the first lesson in a less-controlled activity, and prepares students for the Person to Person activity at the end of the unit.

Time: approximately 15–20 minutes

Person to Person

At the end of each unit, partners work together on a communicative task-based activity based on the functions in the unit. Each partner has information that the other needs to complete the activity, so it is necessary to give and receive information carefully. Students are separated into pairs, and each student reads the information for his or her part according to the instructions in the Student Book.

Expressing personal opinions and ideas, along with active listening, is an important part of this section.

Time: approximately 20–30 minutes

Now Try This

New in this third edition, Now Try This is an extension activity for the Person to Person activity. It can be done by students who finish earlier than their classmates, or it can be done by the whole class to finish off the lesson.

Time: approximately 5 minutes

Optional Activities

Two optional photocopiable activities are provided for each unit. Suggested teaching procedures and answers appear in the back of the Teacher's Book. You may decide to allow for time constraints, student progress, or other pedagogical considerations when presenting them. It is necessary to make copies of the Optional Activity for each student before class.

Time: approximately 15–25 minutes

Review Units

There are four Review Units in the Student Book. The first covers Units 1–3, the second covers the next three units, and so on. Each Review provides students an opportunity to practice the functions through a listening and speaking activity for each unit.

Time: approximately 15–25 minutes per unit

Additional Considerations

Grammar and Usage

Person to Person is not meant to be a grammar text. The authors assume that basic grammar has already been learned and that here the students need practice in using grammar in a natural, conversational setting. However, please note that grammar is carefully controlled so that, as far as possible, the major points of English grammar are reviewed in natural contexts. The units progress in grammatical difficulty, although they can be done out of sequence if the class can handle it. Language Notes, usually found in the Give It a Try sections, contain important grammar and usage explanations. A summary of the grammar points in each unit of the Student Book appears in the Scope and Sequence Chart on pages iii–v.

Pronunciation

Each unit highlights one pronunciation point in the Pronunciation Focus. In addition, other pronunciation points are highlighted in the Teacher's Book. By paying particular attention to these pronunciation points, you will give your students an awareness of those features of American English that will be most useful to them as both listeners and speakers. These pronunciation points are:

sentence stress, intonation, rhythm, blending, and reduction.

Sentence stress and intonation

Speakers use stress and intonation to mark the words they want to highlight, to signal the end of a thought unit, and to indicate such things as whether that unit is part of a series or a completed thought, whether it is a statement, a *Wh-* question, a Yes/No question, or a request.

Intonation Patterns

Speakers of English use various intonation patterns when conversing with others. Here are some examples:

request: Could I have your name, please?

statement: It's Paine.

Wh- question: How do you spell that?

series: It's P-a-i-n-e.

Yes/No question: Do you live in Chicago?

Blending and reduction

Words that are not given strong stress are often said quickly, "swallowed," or otherwise altered. *What did he* becomes /wuh-de/, *could you* becomes /cu-juh/, *did she* becomes /che/, and so on. This is because English is a stress-timed language. In contrast to many languages where speaking each syllable takes the same length of time, English requires *only* those syllables that are stressed to be said slowly. When listening to a rapid stream of speech, students of English sometimes find it hard to recognize even words that they know because they are unfamiliar with their unstressed (or reduced) forms. Part of communicative competence, then, is to be able to recognize reduced forms as well as grasp how stress is used communicatively, such as to highlight important ideas. *Person to Person* addresses these features of pronunciation throughout the Teacher's Book.

General considerations for teaching:

- To heighten students' awareness of the stress, tap out the rhythm or clap your hands, hitting the stressed syllables with greater force. This will also help students see that the rhythm is very even, which is why words get reduced.
- On the board, write intonation and stress patterns with examples.
- Emphasize the pronunciation point as you model the examples given in the Teacher's Book.
- Try to integrate pronunciation work with activities whenever possible. This will help students grasp that control of pronunciation is an essential part of communicative competence. However, during guided practice or role plays it is vital that students be encouraged to develop their fluency and not be interrupted. Pronunciation work should be done either during presentation of a conversation or function, or after the students have completed pair or group work.

Pair Work

Person to Person is based on pair and small-group activities that maximize each student's opportunity to speak in class. Clear language models and guided activities enable pairs to work alone effectively. The elements of real communication are simulated in role plays and information-gap activities. While practicing, it is important to remind students that communication is much more than words. People say a lot with their faces, their gestures, and their tone of voice.

As students practice in pairs or small groups, you can walk around the room and listen to them. In many instances, you will hear incorrect usage, hesitancy, unclear pronunciation, and other areas you may want to work on. It is important, however, not to interrupt the students during free practice. Note the areas that need work and assist the students afterward. Establish yourself as a resource. Encourage students to call on you when they need help.

The procedures mentioned throughout the Teacher's Book are only suggestions. Adapt them in accordance with your own preferences and the particular needs of your students. You will need to experiment to find what works best for your class, keeping in mind that extensive pair work will maximize class time.

Components

Student Book, pages 2–9, 106
Class CD 1, Tracks 2–12
Optional Activities 1.1–1.2,
page 106

Objectives

Functions: Introducing yourself, greeting people, saying good-bye, finding out about people, introducing people

Topics: Greetings, personal information

Structures: *Wh-* questions, *How* questions, *Do* questions, time-of-day expressions

Pronunciation Focus: Pronunciation of *to*

Listen to This: Listening for names and relationships

Student Book page 2

CONSIDER THIS

1. Have students read the information and the questions. Go over any vocabulary students don't know.

2. Group Work. Divide students into groups of four or five. Have students in each group take turns asking and answering the questions. Help students with vocabulary as needed.

3. Ask volunteers to give their answers to the questions.

4. If time allows, discuss naming traditions in the students' cultures. Does the family name come before the first name in an introduction? Is the family name the mother's or father's last name, or both?

Vocabulary

Introduce these words and phrases to the students:

instructor: teacher; someone who shows how to do something

please call me (Bob): used when the speaker wants to be referred to as something other than their given name

terrific: great; fantastic; used to show enthusiasm

Prelistening

1. Pair Work. Have students open their books and look at the photograph. Have partners describe what they see to each other. Circulate and help with vocabulary as needed.

2. Class Work. Read the title of the conversation and the prelistening questions. Ask volunteers to answer the questions.

3. Pair Work. Have pairs list as many women's and men's names in English as they can. Encourage them to think of famous people in sports, movies, music, politics, etc.

4. Class Work. Have pairs read their lists to the class. Make a master list on the board.

Conversation 1

Class CD 1, Track 2

1. With books closed, play the recording or read the conversation.

Bob: Good afternoon.
Eun-mi: Good afternoon.
Bob: I'm your instructor today. My name's Robert Simpson. But please call me Bob.
Eun-mi: Hi, Bob.
Bob: And what's your name?
Eun-mi: I'm Eun-mi.
Bob: Great. And how are you today?
Eun-mi: Fine, thanks.
Bob: Terrific! So let's get started. Are you ready?
Eun-mi: Yeah, let's go!

2. Ask these comprehension questions:

- *Where are the speakers?* (a golf shop)
- *What is the relationship between the two speakers?* (instructor and student)
- *What are they going to do?* (He is going to teach her how to play golf.)

3. Play or read the conversation again, pausing for choral repetition.

4. Ask the following questions:
   - *Is it morning?* (No, it's afternoon.)
   - *What is Speaker 1's name?* (Robert Simpson)
   - *What does Speaker 1 want to be called?* (Bob)
   - *What is Speaker 2's name?* (Eun-mi)
   - *Is Speaker 2 afraid?* (No, she is excited.)

   Elicit responses from various students.

5. Paired Reading. Have students read the conversation, switching roles.

Student Book page 3

Give It a Try

1. Introducing yourself

Presentation

1. Have students look at the function box. Give them time to read the examples.

2. Model the exchanges and have students repeat chorally.

3. Circulate around the room asking students their names.

Notes

1. In the United States, it is very common for people to be referred to by a nickname. A nickname can be a shortened form of the given first name. For example, a person named Jonathan may be called "John," or someone named Margaret may be called "Maggie." A nickname can also refer to the person's apearance or personality. For example, a person with red hair may be called "Red," or someone with a friendly, bright personality might be called "Sunny." Make sure students understand that they should use the name that the person uses to introduce him/herself and not make up their own nickname.

2. Explain to students that a first name is the name given to you at birth by your parents and a last name, or family name, is the name shared by all the members of your family. In the United States, a woman typically changes her last name to her husband's when she marries. However, it is becoming more common for a woman to keep her last name after she marries. When introducing yourself, say your first name first and your family name second.

3. Review intonation of *what* questions. On the board, write:

   What's your <u>name</u>?

   What's your <u>first</u> name?

   What's your <u>last</u> name?

Explain to students that the words that indicate the information that you want are the ones that are stressed. Ask students which words they think will be stressed in these sentences. Mark the stress. Model and have students repeat.

Practice 1

Class CD 1, Track 3

1. Have students read the directions and look at the picture.

2. Play or read the introduction twice.

   A: Hello. My name's Robert. But please call me Bob.

3. Pair work. Have students introduce themselves to each other. Remind them to make eye contact and encourage them to shake hands.

4. Have several pairs demonstrate for the class.

Practice 2

Class CD 1, Track 4

1. Have students read the directions for the activity and look at the picture.

2. Play or read the introduction twice.

   A: My name is Tracy Park. My first name is Tracy. My last name is Park. Please call me Tracy.

3. Divide the class into groups of four or five students.

4. Group Work. Have students take turns introducing themselves to the group.

5. Ask several volunteers to demonstrate for the class.

Extension

1. Class Discussion. Ask the class if any of them have nicknames. Discuss with students if they like their names and if they would prefer to have a nickname.

2. Ask students to give each other nicknames.

Student Book page 4

2. Greeting people

Review. Point to two students and have them introduce themselves to each other. Move quickly around the classroom with other pairs.

Presentation

1. Have students look at the function box. Give them time to read the examples.

2. Model the exchanges and have students repeat chorally.

3. Practice a few exchanges with various students.

Notes

1. Explain to students that greetings can be formal or informal. Discuss with students what situations are formal and informal in their culture and if those situations are different in the United States.

2. Explain to students that *pretty good* is a very common informal response to the question *How are you?* Make sure they understand that the use of *pretty* in this context is not about appearance. It is an adjective that indicates a moderate amount of something.

Practice 1

Class CD 1, Track 5

1. Have students read the directions for the activity.

2. Play or read the example conversations twice.

   1
   A: Hi, Bob.
   B: Hi, Eun-mi.
   A: How are you today?
   B: Fine, thanks. How are you?
   A: Good, thanks.

   2
   C: Good morning.
   D: Hello, Mr. Stevens.

3. Pair Work. Have students take turns introducing themselves to each other.

4. Ask several pairs to demonstrate for the class.

Practice 2

1. Have students read the directions for the activity.

2. Give students time to write their first name on the front of a card and their last name with a title on the back.

3. Group Work. Have students show the back of the card and take turns introducing themselves formally to the group. Then have them turn the cards over and introduce themselves informally.

4. Ask several volunteers to demonstrate for the class.

3. Saying good-bye

Presentation

1. Have students look at the function box. Give them time to read the examples.

2. Model the exchanges and have students repeat chorally.

3. Practice a few exchanges with various students.

Practice

Class CD 1, Track 6

1. Have students read the directions for the activity.

2. Play or read the example conversations twice.

   1
   A: OK. See you later.
   B: Yeah, see you.

   2
   A: Well, nice talking to you. Good-bye.
   B: Good-bye.

3. Pair Work. Have students take turns saying good-bye to one another.

4. Ask several pairs to demonstrate for the class.

Extension

Have the class brainstorm different situations where they would have to introduce themselves. Choose two students and point to one of the situations on the board. Have the students say if the situation is formal or informal and then role-play an appropriate introduction. Continue with other pairs.

Student Book page 5

Listen to This

Class CD 1, Track 7

Part 1

1. Have students read the directions and look at the chart. Make sure they understand the headings. To check comprehension ask: *Which columns will you look at for this activity?* (the first and second columns)

2. Play or read the conversations. Tell students to check the correct column.

   1
   W: Hi, Cheng-han. How are things?
   C: Pretty good, thanks. And you?
   W: Fine, thanks. How was your weekend?
   C: Great, thanks. How about you?
   W: It was OK. Oh, it's time for class. See you.
   C: Yeah. Have a nice day.

   2
   S: Hey, Jean. Good to see you again.
   J: Hi, Simon. How are things?
   S: Good, thanks. How are you?
   J: Fine, thanks.
   S: Are you going downtown?
   J: Yes, I am. Bye.
   S: Bye-bye.

3

B: Good evening. I'm Brian Baxter.
T: Hello. I'm Ted Ozaki.
B: Nice to meet you, Ted.
T: Are you from the States?
B: No, I'm Canadian, from Toronto.
T: That's a great city.
B: Yeah. Well, nice talking to you.
T: See you again.

4

P: Hello. My name's Pei-ling.
M: Nice to meet you.
P: Say, are you in my Spanish class?
M: No, I'm taking Korean.
P: Oh, yeah? Class starts at 11, doesn't it?
M: That's right. See you later.

3. Play or read the conversations again as students check their answers.

4. Ask volunteers to say which column they checked for each conversation so students can check their work.

Answers:
1. friends
2. friends
3. first time
4. first time

Part 2

1. Have students read the directions. To check comprehension ask: *Which column will you look at for this activity?* (How did it end?)

2. Play or read the conversations again. Tell students to listen for how each conversation ends.

3. Play or read the conversation again for students to check their answers.

4. Ask volunteers for their answers.

Answers:
1. Have a nice day.
2. Bye-bye.
3. See you again.
4. See you later.

Part 3

1. Have students read the directions. Play or read the conversations again, if necessary.

2. Ask volunteers for their answers and the reasons for their answers.

Possible Answer:
The people seem to know each other best in Conversation 1, which has more informal language, and least in Conversation 3, which uses the most formal language.

Let's Talk

Part 1

1. Have students read the directions and the questions in the chart. Go over vocabulary students don't know.

2. To check comprehension, ask a few volunteers to answer the questions in the chart.

3. Have students write their answers in the first column. Circulate and help as needed.

Part 2

1. Have students read the directions and look at the example conversation.

2. Divide the class into groups of four. Have students introduce themselves.

3. Group Work. Have students take turns asking and answering questions to fill in the chart. Circulate and help as needed.

4. Have someone from each group report some of the group's answers to the class.

Do you want to meet him?

Student Book page 6

Vocabulary

Introduce these words and phrases to the students:

guy: an informal word for *man*

aerobics: a kind of exercise

cute: an informal word for handsome or pretty

You bet I do!: an informal way to express enthusiastic agreement

Prelistening

1. Have students open their books and look at the photograph. Ask:

   - *Where are the speakers?* (in a coffee shop)
   - *What do you think they are talking about?* (the man in the coffee shop)

2. Pair Work. Read the title of the conversation and the prelistening questions. Have students take turns asking and answering the questions.

3. Class Work. Have pairs share their answers with the class.

Note

Explain to students that in the United States it is common for friends to "fix up" or "set up" their single male and female friends if they think they would like each other.

Conversation 2

Class CD 1, Track 8

1. With books closed, play the recording or read the conversation.

Nishi:	Who's that guy?
Eun-mi:	That's Tony.
Nishi:	Who's he?
Eun-mi:	Oh, he's in my aerobics class.
Nishi:	He's really cute.
Eun-mi:	Yeah. Do you want to meet him?
Nishi:	You bet I do!
Eun-mi:	Tony, this is my friend, Nishi.
Tony:	Hi, Nishi. Nice to meet you.
Nishi:	Hello. Nice to meet you, too.

2. Ask this comprehension question:

   - *What is the relationship between the two speakers?* (friends)

3. Say: *Listen again. This time listen to the details of the conversation.*

4. Play or read the conversation again, pausing for choral repetition. Allow students to write down the information as they listen. Play or read the conversation again, if needed, for students to get all the information.

5. Ask the following questions:

   - *Does Speaker 1 know the man in the coffee shop?* (no)
   - *Does Speaker 2 know him?* (yes)
   - *What is his name?* (Tony)
   - *How does Speaker 2 know him?* (from aerobics class)
   - *What does Speaker 1 think about him?* (that he's cute)
   - *Does Speaker 1 want to meet him?* (yes)
   - *What is Speaker 1's name?* (Nishi)

Elicit responses from various students.

PRONUNCIATION FOCUS

Class CD 1, Track 9

1. Explain what the focus is. Play or read the examples in the book and have students repeat chorally.

   Do you want to meet him?
   Nice to meet you.

2. With books open, play or read the conversation again. Tell students to pay attention to the pronunciation of the word *to*.

3. Paired Reading. Have students practice the conversation, switching roles.

Give It a Try

1. Finding out about people

Presentation

1. Have students look at the function box. Give them time to read the examples.

2. Model the exchanges and have students repeat chorally.

3. Practice a few exchanges with various students.

Practice 1

Class CD 1, Track 10

1. Have students read the directions and look at the picture.

2. Play or read the example conversation twice.

   A: Who's that guy?
   B: That's Tony. Who's she?
   A: That's Nishi.

3. Have students look at the word box. Read each phrase and have students repeat chorally. Help with vocabulary as needed.

4. Pair Work. Give students ten seconds to look at the names under each picture. Tell them to cover the names. Have them take turns asking and answering questions about the people and their names.

5. Have several pairs demonstrate their conversations for the class.

Practice 2

1. Have students read the directions.

2. Pair Work. Have students take turns asking and answering questions about their classmates' names.

3. Have several pairs demonstrate their conversations for the class.

Extension

Cut out pictures of individual people from magazines and tape them to the board. Adjust the number of pictures depending on the level of your class. Write a name under each picture. Give students ten seconds to memorize the names. Divide the class into pairs and have each pair use the examples from Practice 1 to ask and answer questions about the names and write them all down. The first pair to get all the names correct wins.

2. Introducing people

Presentation

1. Have students look at the function box. Give them time to read the examples.

2. Model the exchanges and have students repeat chorally.

3. Practice a few exchanges with various students.

Notes

1. Explain to students that when being introduced to someone, it is very important to shake hands, smile, and look the person in the eye. If time allows, practice shaking hands and making introductions with students.

2. On the board, write the following statements and mark the intonation:

   Tony, this is my friend, Nishi.

   Tom, I'd like you to meet Bob.

   Model the examples and have students repeat.

Practice 1

Class CD 1, Track 11

1. Have students read the directions and look at the list.

2. Play or read the example conversation twice.

   A: Tony, this is my friend, Nishi.
   B: Hi, Nishi. Nice to meet you.
   C: Hi. Nice to meet you, too.

3. Model the activity by getting one student to play Marie and one to play Ricardo. Say: *Marie, this is my classmate Ricardo.* Prompt the other students' responses if necessary.

4. Group Work. Divide the class into groups of three. Have students take turns introducing one person (Marie) to another person (from the list).

5. Have several groups demonstrate their introductions to the class.

Practice 2

1. Have students read the directions.

2. Divide students into groups of three or four.

3. Group Work. Have students take turns introducing one of the students to the others in the group.

4. Have several groups demonstrate their introductions to the class.

Listen to This

Class CD 1, Track 12

Part 1

1. Have students read the directions and look at the chart. Make sure students understand what each heading means.

2. To check comprehension, ask: *Which columns will you look at for this activity?* (the first and second columns)

3. Play or read the conversations. Tell students to check the correct column for each conversation.

1
M: Who's that guy?
P: Oh, that's Johnny Chen. He's a good friend of mine. Don't you know him?
M: No, I don't.
P: Really? Hey, Johnny!
J: Hi, guys.
P: Johnny. This is Maya.
J: Hi, Maya. Nice to meet you.
M: Nice to meet you, too.

2
M: Who's that woman with the red hair?
P: That's Sandra.
M: Is she in your class?
P: No, she's my neighbor.
M: Really?
P: Yeah. Let me introduce you. She's really nice.
M: OK.
P: Oh, Sandra. This is Maya.
S: Hi, Maya. Nice to meet you.
M: Yeah, you too.

3
M: Who's that man?
P: Oh, that's my Japanese teacher, Mr. Okano.
M: Really. Is he from Tokyo?
P: No, he's from Sapporo. Let's talk to him. Good morning, Mr. Okano.
O: *Ohayō gozaimasu*, Phillip.
P: Mr. Okano. I'd like you to meet my friend Maya.
O: Hello, Maya. Nice to meet you.
M: Nice to meet you, too.

4
M: Is that one of your teachers?
P: No, she's in my computer class. She's really nice. Do you want to meet her?
M: Sure.
P: Oh, Ms. Ford. I'd like you to meet my friend Maya.
F: How do you do?
M: Nice to meet you.

4. Pair work. Play or read the conversations again as students check each other's answers.

5. Ask several students for their answers.

> **Answers:**
> 1. informal
> 2. informal
> 3. formal
> 4. formal

Part 2

1. Have students read the directions.

2. To check comprehension, ask: *Which columns will you look at for this activity?* (the last four)

3. Play or read the conversations again and tell students to listen for the relationship between the speaker and the person he/she is introducing.

4. Play or read the conversations again for students to check their answers.

5. Ask volunteers for their answers.

> **Answers:**
> 1. friend
> 2. neighbor
> 3. teacher
> 4. classmate

Part 3

1. Have students read the directions.

2. Pair Work. Have students discuss which conversations were formal and which were informal.

3. Have several pairs report the results of their conversations to the class.

Extension

Have pairs write their own examples of a formal and informal conversation and introduction. Then have them perform them for the class.

Person to Person

Part 1

1. Divide the class into groups of four and have groups decide who will be Students A, B, C, and D. Remind Students C and D to turn to page 106.

2. Have students read the instructions.

3. Pair Work. Tell students to introduce themselves and record their information, including their title *(Mr./Ms./Mrs./Miss)*.

Part 2

1. Have students read the directions.

2. Group Work. Have an A/B pair join a C/D pair, and introduce their partner to the other pair. Have students record information about the new pair.

3. Have several groups demonstrate for the class.

Now Try This

1. Have students read the directions.

2. Group Work. Have each original pair join up with a new pair. Have each pair take turns introducing their partner to the other pair.

3. Have several groups demonstrate for the class.

Extension

On separate slips of paper, write down various situations (meeting a new classmate, meeting your new boss, etc.) and different names (Jane, Mrs. Robert Robertson, etc.). Have a student choose a name and a situation and role-play making an appropriate introduction.

Unit 2   Are these your keys?

Components

Student Book, pages 10–17, 107
Class CD 1, Tracks 13–22
Optional Activities 2.1–2.2,
pages 106–107

Objectives

Functions: Identifying things, complimenting people, describing where things are, asking where things are

Topics: Clothing, everyday items, describing items, describing the location of items

Structures: *Do* questions, *Wh-* questions, possessive *s*, possessive pronouns, prepositions of location

Pronunciation Focus: Pronunciation of [s] at the end of a noun

Listen to This: Listening for where items are located

Student Book page 10

CONSIDER THIS

1. Have students read the information and the questions. Go over any vocabulary students don't know.

2. Group Work. Divide students into groups of four or five. Have students in each group take turns asking and answering the questions. Help students with vocabulary as needed.

3. Have volunteers tell the class about the things they never leave home without.

Vocabulary

Introduce these words and phrases to the students:

cell phone: short for cellular telephone

wow: an expression of surprise

neat: an informal way to express satisfaction

cool: an informal way to express satisfaction

by the way: an interjection that signals the speaker is changing the subject

Prelistening

1. Pair Work. Have students open their books and look at the photograph. Have partners describe what they see. Circulate and help with vocabulary as needed.

2. Class Work. Read the title of the conversation and the prelistening questions. Ask volunteers to answer the questions.

3. Pair Work. Have students discuss the questions and take notes on their partner's answers.

4. Class Work. Have pairs report on each other's answers.

Conversation 1

Class CD 1, Track 13

1. With books closed, play the recording or read the conversation.

   Emily: What's that?
   Akemi: It's my new cell phone.
   Emily: Wow. It's really small.
   Akemi: Yeah. And listen.
   Emily: That's neat. And I like your sunglasses. They're cool.
   Akemi: Thanks.
   Emily: By the way, are these your keys?
   Akemi: Oh, yes. They are mine. Thanks. Sorry, I leave my things everywhere!
   Emily: I know. Here's your notebook.

2. Ask these comprehension questions:

   • *What is the relationship between the two speakers?* (friends)
   • *Are the speakers talking about something serious or casual?* (casual)

3. Play or read the conversation again, pausing for choral repetition.

4. Ask the following questions:
   - *What does Speaker 1 ask Speaker 2 about first?* (her cell phone)
   - *Is the cell phone big or small?* (small)
   - *Is it old or new?* (new)
   - *What does Speaker 1 comment about next?* (Speaker 2's sunglasses)
   - *What does Speaker 1 ask Speaker 2 about next?* (her keys)
   - *What else does Speaker 2 forget?* (her notebook)

   Elicit responses from various students.

5. Paired Reading. Have students read the conversation, switching roles.

Student Book page 11

Give It a Try

1. Identifying things (1)

Presentation

1. Have students look at the function box. Give them time to read the examples.

2. Model the exchanges and have students repeat chorally.

3. Practice a few exchanges with various students.

Notes

1. Make sure students understand how distance relates to the usage of *these/those* and *that/this*. Demonstrate with various objects around the class that are close to you and far from you. For example, *This is a pencil. That is a desk.* Then have several volunteers make their own examples.

2. Review pronunciation of [th]. Demonstrate proper placement of the tongue firmly against the back of the teeth.

3. Remind students that when asking a question, tone is very important. Demonstrate a polite tone and an impolite tone using these questions:

   What's that?

   What are those?

Practice

Class CD 1, Track 14

1. Have students read the directions for the activity and look at the picture and the list of items. Go over any vocabulary students don't know. Ask volunteers to say if each item is singular or plural.

2. Play or read the example conversation twice.

   A: What's this?
   B: It's my cell phone.
   A: What are these?
   B: They're earrings.

3. Pair Work. Have pairs take turns asking each other about the items in the picture. Circulate and help as needed.

4. Ask several pairs to demonstrate for the class.

2. Identifying things (2)

Presentation

1. Have students look at the function box. Give them time to read the examples.

2. Model the exchanges and have students repeat chorally.

3. Practice a few exchanges with various students.

Practice 1

Class CD 1, Track 15

1. Have students read the directions for the activity. Students may look briefly at the picture of the two students before covering it. Have students look at the pictures of the items. Review vocabulary, if needed. Ask volunteers to say if each item is singular or plural.

2. Play or read the example conversation twice.

   A: Whose earrings are these?
   B: They're Karen's.

3. Pair Work. Have pairs take turns asking each other if the items are Paul's or Karen's. Circulate and help as needed.

4. Ask volunteers for the answers.

Practice 2

1. Have students read the directions for the activity. Give them time to come up with the four items they will put on the desk. Circulate and help with vocabulary, if needed.

2. Group Work. Divide students into groups and have each group sit around the same desk. Have them put their four items on the desk at the same time. Give each student ten seconds to try and state who each item belongs to.

   These are Keiko's sunglasses. This is Alicia's ring. I think this is Tony's pen…

3. Ask a member of each group to identify all the items for the class.

Extension

Bring in pictures from magazines that have many objects in them. Have pairs of students take turns asking and answering questions about the objects in the picture. Have students use their dictionaries to make lists of new words in the picture.

3. Complimenting people

Review. Point to a student and then to an object in the classroom. Elicit the question *What (is/are) (this/that/these/those)?* Point to another student to answer. Move quickly around the classroom.

Presentation

1. Have students look at the function box. Give them time to read the examples.

2. Model the exchanges and have students repeat chorally.

3. Practice a few exchanges with various students.

Note

Explain to students that it is nice to pay someone a compliment, but they should be careful about not making compliments too personal. Saying that someone looks nice in a particular color is fine, but making a comment, even a positive one, about someone's body is inappropriate.

Practice

Class CD 1, Track 16

1. Have students read the directions for the activity and look at the words in the word box. Go over any vocabulary they don't know.

2. Play or read the example twice.

   A: Hi, Jim.
   B: Hi, Kumiko.
   A: How are things?
   B: Pretty good, thanks.
   A: Oh, I like your T-shirt. It's cool.
   B: Thanks. And that's a nice watch.
   A: Thanks. Well, see you later.
   B: Bye.

3. Have students look at the word box. Read each word and have students repeat chorally. Help with vocabulary as needed. Make sure students understand the shades of meaning for each word.

4. Class Work. Have students move around the classroom and greet each other. Have them take turns giving each other a compliment about something they are wearing.

5. Ask several pairs to demonstrate for the class.

Extension

Have students use their dictionaries to add words to the Use These Words list.

Listen to This

Class CD 1, Track 17

Part 1

1. Have students read the directions and look at the choices. Make sure they understand the possible answers.

2. Play or read the conversation. Tell students to check the correct choice.

   S: Hey, Amanda. Could you help me sort the clothes?
   A: Sure. Are these your socks, Suzie?
   S: Yeah, they're mine. Thanks.
   A: What about these jeans? Are they yours or mine?
   S: Let me see. Oh, they're too small for me. They're yours.
   A: OK. And this T-shirt is mine, too. But I think this top is yours. Take a look.
   S: Yep. That's mine.
   A: Pass me the dress. That's mine. But not the shorts.
   S: Yeah, they're mine. But not the scarf. Here.
   A: Thanks.
   S: That's funny. Where are my pants?
   A: Hmm…They're not here. And I can't find my gloves or my jacket.
   S: Oh, here's your jacket. But your gloves aren't here.

3. Play or read the conversation again for students to check their answers.

4. Ask volunteers for their answers.

Answer:
at the laundromat

Part 2

1. Have students read the directions and look at the clothing items. Go over any vocabulary students don't know.

2. To check comprehension, ask *If the shorts are Amanda's, what will you write and where will you write it?* (an A next to *shorts*)

3. Play or read the conversation again and tell students to listen for which item of clothing belongs to whom.

4. Play or read the conversation again for students to check their answers.

5. Ask volunteers for their answers.

Answers:
S: socks, top, shorts
A: T-shirt, jacket, scarf, dress, jeans

Part 3

1. Have students read the directions for the activity and have them look at the pictures and the example conversation.

2. Pair Work. Have pairs take turns pointing to items and saying to whom each one belongs.

3. Ask several pairs to give their answers.

Let's Talk

Part 1

1. Have students read the directions and look at the pictures. Ask for a volunteer and model the activity using the example conversation.

2. Pair Work. Have students work together to identify each of the items pictured. Circulate and help as needed.

Part 2

1. Have students read the directions and look at the pictures. Ask for a volunteer and model the activity using the example conversation.

2. Have students get together with another partner. Have them look at the sample conversation and take turns asking and answering questions about the items and who they belong to.

3. Ask volunteers to share their conversations with the class.

Part 3

1. Have students read the directions.

2. Pair Work. Have students talk about which items they have. Encourage students to expand on the conversation as much as they can. For example, they should try to talk about when they bought the item, what it looks like, whether they like it or not, and how and when they use it.

3. Have several students report on their partner's answers.

Where are they?

Vocabulary

Introduce these words and phrases to the students:

late: not on time

dresser: a piece of furniture with drawers in which clothing is kept

sofa: another word for couch

Prelistening

1. Have students open their books and look at the photograph. Ask:

   - *Where are the speakers?* (in their home)
   - *What do you think is happening?* (The woman is late.)

2. Pair Work. Read the title of the conversation and the prelistening questions. Have students take turns asking and answering the questions.

3. Class Work. Have pairs share their answers with the class.

Notes

1. Teach students words such as *forgetful*, *absent-minded*, *scatter-brained*.

2. Review with students objects that seem to be singular but grammatically are plural, for example, *scissors*, *pants*, and *glasses*.

Conversation 2

Class CD 1, Track 18

1. With books closed, play the recording or read the conversation.

   Akemi: Oh, I'm late again. Where are my car keys?
   Taro: Are they in the drawer?
   Akemi: No, they're not.
   Taro: Oh, I know. They're in the bedroom, on the dresser.
   Akemi: Great. Now where is my bag?
   Taro: There, on the sofa next to the pillow.
   Akemi: Good. Oh, but where are my glasses?
   Taro: You're wearing them!
   Akemi: You're right!

2. Ask this comprehension question:

   - *What is Speaker 1's problem?* (She's late and she can't find her things.)

3. Say: *Listen again. This time listen to the details of the conversation.*

4. Play or read the conversation again, pausing for choral repetition. Allow students to write down the information as they listen. Play or read the conversation again, if needed, for students to get all the information.

5. Ask the following questions:

   - *Is this the first time Speaker 1 has been late?* (no)
   - *How do you know?* (She says she is late again.)
   - *Where does Speaker 2 think the keys are at first?* (in the drawer)
   - *Are they there?* (no)
   - *Where are the keys?* (in the bedroom on the dresser)
   - *What is the next thing that Speaker 1 can't find?* (her bag)
   - *Where is the bag?* (next to the sofa)
   - *What is the next thing Speaker 1 can't find?* (her glasses)
   - *Where are the glasses?* (She's wearing them.)

   Elicit responses from various students.

PRONUNCIATION FOCUS

Class CD 1, Track 19

1. Explain what the focus is. Write the examples on the board, along with the headings. Play or read the examples and have students repeat chorally.

[s]	[z]	[iz]
books	keys	glasses

2. With books open, play or read the conversation again. Tell students to pay attention to the pronunciation of the example words on the board.

3. Paired Reading. Have students practice the conversation, switching roles.

Give It a Try

1. Describing where things are

Presentation

1. Have students look at the function box and the pictures and labels. Give them time to read the examples.

2. Model the exchanges and have students repeat chorally.

3. Practice a few exchanges with various students, using each of the phrases below the pictures.

Practice 1

Class CD 1, Track 20

1. Have students read the directions and look at the picture and list of items.

2. Play or read the example conversation twice.

   A: Where are my keys?
   B: They're in the bedroom.
   A: Where's my book?
   B: It's next to the sofa.

3. Pair Work. Have students take turns asking and answering questions about where the items are in the picture.

4. Have several pairs demonstrate their conversations for the class.

Practice 2

1. Have students read the directions.

2. Pair Work. Have students take turns talking about the location of five other items in the picture.

3. Have volunteers demonstrate for the class.

Extension

Divide the class into two or three teams. Have one student from each team think of an object in the classroom and turn their back to the other students. Then have that student describe the location of the object. The first team to call out the correct object wins a point for their team. Set a time limit or a point limit. Alternatively, write classroom objects on separate slips of paper and put them in a bag. Have one student pick one of the objects out of the bag and describe its location. Make sure students do not look at the object and give away its location to the other students.

2. Asking where things are

Presentation

1. Have students look at the function box. Give them time to read the examples.

2. Model the exchanges and have students repeat chorally.

3. Practice a few exchanges with various students.

Note

Remind students that stress is given to the content words in a sentence. Content words are the nouns, verbs, adjectives, and adverbs. These words are said louder and held longer. Other parts of a sentence, such as auxiliary verbs, articles, pronouns, and prepositions, are usually not stressed. On the board write the following sentences:

   Is the <u>newspaper</u> on the <u>table</u>?

   Are the <u>magazines</u> on the <u>sofa</u>?

   Is the <u>book</u> under the <u>table</u>?

   Are the <u>glasses</u> next to the <u>book</u>?

Have volunteers go to the board and mark the content words in each sentence. Model the sentences and have students repeat.

Practice 1

Class CD 1, Track 21

1. Have students read the directions and look at the picture and the list of items. Go over any vocabulary students don't know.

2. Play or read the example twice.

   A: Is the newspaper on the table?
   B: Yes, it is.
   A: Are the magazines on the sofa?
   B: No, they aren't. They're on the table.

3. Pair Work. Have students take turns asking and answering questions about the location of the items in the picture.

4. Have several pairs demonstrate their conversations to the class.

Practice 2

1. Have students read the directions and look at the example.

2. Pair Work. Have students take turns asking and answering questions about items in the classroom.

3. Have several pairs demonstrate their conversations to the class.

Listen to This

Class CD 1, Track 22

Part 1

1. Have students read the directions and look at the choices. Make sure they remember what *misplaced* means.

2. Play the recording or read the conversation. Tell students to put a ✓ only next to the misplaced items that are mentioned in the conversation, not all the items mentioned.

   A: I'm looking for my cell phone.
   B: It's over there, on top of the bookshelf.
   A: Right. And what about my camera?
   B: Look. There it is. On top of the TV. And your wallet is next to the TV if you're looking for it.
   A: Of course.
   B: Where are those magazines I was reading, by the way?
   A: Oh, I put them in the drawer.
   B: OK. And my watch is here, too. But my sunglasses. Did you see them?
   A: Yeah. They're on the floor, next to the sofa. See?
   B: Oh, yeah.
   A: And where are my shoes?
   B: There, in front of the bookshelf.
   A: OK. And where did I put my briefcase?
   B: It's under the table.

A: What about the remote control?
B: It's on the sofa.
A: And one more thing. Where is my tennis racket?
B: It's behind the door.

3. Play or read the conversation again for students to check their answers.

4. Ask volunteers for the answers.

> **Answers:**
> cell phone, camera, sunglasses, shoes, briefcase, wallet, tennis racket, remote control, magazines

Part 2

1. Have students read the directions and look at the chart.

2. Play or read the conversation again and tell students to write the location of each item in the chart.

3. Play the conversation again for students to check their answers.

4. Ask volunteers for their answers.

> **Answers:**
> 1. on top of the bookshelf
> 2. on top of the TV
> 3. in front of the bookshelf
> 4. under the table

Part 3

1. Have students read the directions and look at the chart.

2. Play or read the conversation again and tell students to write which items are at the locations in the chart.

3. Ask volunteers for their answers.

> **Answers:**
> 1. wallet
> 2. tennis racket
> 3. magazines; watch

Person to Person

Part 1

1. Divide the class into pairs and have students decide who will be Student A and who will be Student B. Remind Student B to look at page 107.

2. Have students read the instructions and look at their picture and the example conversation.

3. Pair Work. Have students take turns asking and answering questions about each other's pictures without looking at their partner's picture. Tell them to write down the differences that they find. Circulate and help as needed.

Part 2

1. Have students read the directions and look at the example.

2. Pair Work. Put each Student A with a different Student B than in Part 1. Have students compare their list of differences with their new partner.

3. Ask several students for their answers.

Now Try This

1. Have students read the directions.

2. Pair Work. Have students work in pairs to write four true statements and two false statements about things in the classroom.

3. Group Work. Put students into groups of two pairs. Have pairs take turns reading their statements and saying if each statement is true or false.

4. Have groups read a few of their sentences to the class.

Extension

Have students draw their own pictures of a room or a scene on a large piece of paper. Divide the class into groups of four. Have students describe their pictures to the group.

Unit 3

How old are you?

Components

Student Book, pages 18–25, 108
Class CD 1, Tracks 23–32
Optional Activities 3.1–3.2,
page 107

Objectives

Functions: Describing personal information, talking about interests, talking and asking about family members

Topics: Physical descriptions, hobbies and interests, family information

Structures: *Wh-* questions, *How* questions, Yes/No questions, *Tell me about…*

Pronunciation Focus: Question intonation

Listen to This: Listening for someone's interests and family

Student Book page 18

CONSIDER THIS

1. Have students read the information and the questions. Go over any vocabulary students don't know.

2. Group Work. Divide students into groups of four or five. Have students in each group take turns asking and answering the questions. Help students with vocabulary as needed.

3. Ask volunteers to give their answers to the questions.

Vocabulary

Introduce this word to the students:

(sports) club: a group of people with the same interests

Note

Explain to students that in the United States clubs are very popular in high school and college.

Prelistening

1. Pair Work. Have students open their books and look at the photograph. Have partners describe what they see to each other. Circulate and help with vocabulary as needed.

2. Class Work. Read the title of the conversation and the prelistening questions. Ask volunteers to answer the questions.

3. Pair work. Have pairs list the sports they enjoy and discuss whether height, weight, or age are important.

4. Ask volunteers to answer the questions.

Conversation 1

Class CD 1, Track 23

1. With books closed, play the recording or read the conversation.

   Fu-An: I think I'd like to join the sports club.
   Malik: Great. Let me ask you a few questions. How old are you?
   Fu-an: I'm 19.
   Malik: And how tall are you?
   Fu-an: I'm 180 cm.
   Malik: OK. One more thing. How much do you weigh?
   Fu-an: I weigh 70 kilos.
   Malik: And what kinds of sports are you interested in?
   Fu-an: I like all team sports, and I also like swimming.

2. Ask these comprehension questions:

   • *Where are the speakers?* (at a school club fair or event where students learn about and join clubs)
   • *What does Speaker 1 want to do?* (join the sports club)

3. Play or read the conversation again, pausing for choral repetition.

4. Ask the following questions:
   - *How old is Speaker 1?* (19)
   - *What is the second question Speaker 2 asks?* (How tall are you?)
   - *How tall is Speaker 1?* (180 cm)
   - *What is the third question Speaker 2 asks?* (How much do you weigh?)
   - *How much does Speaker 1 weigh?* (70 kilos)
   - *What is the last question Speaker 2 asks?* (What kinds of sports are you interested in?)
   - *What sports does Speaker 1 like?* (all team sports and swimming)

   Elicit responses from various students.

5. Paired Reading. Have students read the conversation, switching roles.

Student Book page 19

Give It a Try

1. Describing personal information

Presentation

1. Have students look at the function box. Give them time to read the examples.

2. Model the exchanges and have students repeat chorally.

3. Practice a few exchanges with various students.

Notes

1. Explain to students that in the United States it is inappropriate to ask about someone's physical characteristics in everyday conversation. This information is only asked for in specific types of situations, such as a doctor's exam or when applying for a driver's license.

2. Explain to students that in the United States the metric system is not widely used. Weight is measured in pounds, height in feet and inches. One foot equals 30.48 centimeters, one inch equals 2.54 centimeters, and one kilogram equals 2.2 pounds.

Practice 1

Class CD 1, Track 24

1. Have students read the directions for the activity and look at the chart.

2. Play or read the example conversation twice.

   A: How old are you?
   B: I'm 18.
   A: How tall are you?
   B: I'm 172 centimeters tall.

3. Group Work. Have students take turns asking and answering each other about their name, age, and height. Circulate and help as needed.

4. Have a student from each group report their group's information to the class.

Practice 2

1. Have students read the directions for the activity and look at the example.

2. Class Work. Have students take turns reading the age and height information in their chart and asking the class whose information it is.

Extension

Have the class brainstorm situations in which they would have to give their personal information. Write the situations on the board. Divide the class into pairs and have each pair write their own role play using one of the situations on the board. Have each pair present their role play to the class.

Student Book page 20

2. Talking about interests (1)

Review. Have a student describe themselves by saying their height, weight, and age. Move quickly around the classroom.

Presentation

1. Have students look at the function box. Give them time to read the examples.

2. Model the exchanges and have students repeat chorally.

3. Practice a few exchanges with various students.

Practice 1

1. Have students read the directions and look at the chart. Give students time to add their own ideas to the chart.

2. To check comprehension, ask a volunteer: *Are you interested in baseball?* Have them answer and then ask: *If yes, where will you check? If no, will you check anything?*

3. Have students put a ✔ next to the activities they are interested in.

Practice 2

Class CD 1, Track 25

1. Have students read the directions and look at the word box. Read each word or phrase and have students repeat chorally. Help with vocabulary as needed.

2. To check comprehension, ask a volunteer: *What will you ask your partner?* Have them answer and then ask: *Where will you check their yes answers?*

3. Play or read the example conversation twice.

   A: Are you interested in sports?
   B: Sure.
   A: What kind of sports are you interested in?
   B: I like swimming.

4. Pair Work. Have students take turns asking and answering questions about the sports they are interested in.

5. Have pairs report on their partner's interests to the class.

3. Talking about interests (2)

Presentation

1. Have students look at the function box. Give them time to read the examples.

2. Model the exchanges and have students repeat chorally.

3. Practice a few exchanges with various students.

Practice 1

Class CD 1, Track 26

1. Have students read the directions and look at the list of activities and the words in the box. Go over any vocabulary they don't know.

2. Give students time to check their interests.

3. Play or read the example conversation twice.

   A: Are you interested in movies?
   B: Yeah.
   A: What kind?
   B: I like comedies.

4. Pair Work. Have students take turns asking and answering questions about their interests.

5. Have pairs report their partner's answers to the class.

Extension

1. Have students use their dictionaries to add words to the Use These Words list.

2. Have the class vote on the most popular interests. If possible, discuss with students why they enjoy those interests and how and when they pursue their interests.

Student Book page 21

Listen to This

Class CD 1, Track 27

Part 1

1. Have students read the directions and look at the choices.

2. Play the recording or read the conversations. Tell students to write the number of the conversation next to the correct choice.

   1
   A: What are you doing on Saturday, David?
   D: I want to watch the school baseball game. I love baseball.
   A: Me too. What other sports do you like?
   D: Tennis is my other favorite sport.
   A: And do you play basketball?
   D: Sure.
   A: I thought so. You are really tall. How tall are you?
   D: I'm 178 cms.
   A: Wow. And you're only 14 years old!

   2
   A: Are you going to join the drama club this semester, Meena?
   M: I don't think so. I want to play more sports. I'm going to join the sports club.
   A: Great. What sports do you like?
   M: Volleyball and basketball. I'm kind of short for both games, but it doesn't matter. I love them.
   A: So how tall are you?
   M: 169 cm.
   A: And how old are you?
   M: Nineteen.

   3
   A: Are you going to play baseball on Saturday, Sandra?
   S: No, I need some new sneakers. I'm going downtown to look for some. I also need a new tennis racket.
   A: So you're good at baseball *and* tennis? Fantastic! And you're only 18.
   S: I also play volleyball.
   A: Wow! Are you the tallest person on the team?
   S: No, I'm 180 cm, but Julia is 187 cm.

3. Play or read the conversations again for students to check their answers.

4. Ask volunteers for their answers.

Answers:
2, 1, 3

Part 2

Listen again. Complete the chart.

1. Have students read the directions and look at the chart.

2. Play or read the conversations again and tell students to listen for the age, height, and sports interests of each person. Have students fill in the chart.

4. Play or read the conversation again for students to check their answers.

5. Ask volunteers for their answers.

> **Answers:**
> David: 14/178 cm/baseball; tennis; basketball
> Meena: 19/169 cm/volleyball; basketball
> Sandra: 18/180 cm/baseball; tennis; volleyball

Part 3

1. Have students read the directions and look at the sports they wrote in the third column.

2. Play or read the conversation again if necessary.

3. Pair Work. Have students take turns asking and answering questions about the different people's sports interests.

4. Have volunteers report to the class.

Let's Talk

Part 1

1. Have students read the directions and look at the chart. Brainstorm with the class things they can put in the last column heading (video games, cooking, fashion, etc.).

2. Have students write their information in the chart. To check comprehension, ask: *Where will you write your height?*

3. Circulate and help as needed.

Part 2

1. Have students read the directions. To check comprehension, ask a few students: *What is one question you will ask another student in your group?*

2. Group Work. Divide students into groups of four. Have them take turns asking and answering questions about their personal information and interests. Have them fill in the chart. (Students may wish to reproduce the chart in a larger form in their notebooks so they have more room to write classmates' answers.)

Part 3

1. Have students read the directions.

2. Class Work. Have students report to the class on who had similar interests in their group.

Extension

Discuss with students which activities seem to be the most popular and why. Talk about who has the most unusual interests. Ask students about what other interests they would like to pursue but can't because of time, money, etc.

Tell me about your family.

Student Book page 22

Vocabulary

Introduce these words and phrases to the students:

medium-sized: not big, but not small

What do (your parents) do?: a way to ask what someone's occupation is

engineer: someone involved in the design and construction of buildings and structures

pharmacist: someone who sells medicine and understands their use

Prelistening

1. Have students open their books and look at the photograph. Ask students:
   - *Where are the speakers?* (in a classroom)

2. Class Work. Read the title of the conversation and the prelistening questions. Have students take turns asking and answering the questions.

3. Class Work. Have pairs share their answers with the class.

Notes

1. Teach students family words such as *niece, nephew, aunt, uncle, cousin, sibling, in-law, nuclear family, immediate family, extended family*, etc., depending on the level of your class.

2. Explain to students that English-speaking cultures have relatively few family terms. For example, there are no separate terms for older or younger sister or brother and no terms for female or male cousin. If time allows, discuss how this is different from the students' own cultures.

Conversation 2

Class CD 1, Track 28

1. With books closed, play the recording or read the conversation.

   Fu-an: So, Eva. Tell me about your family.
   Eva: Well, I come from a medium-sized family.
   Fu-an: How many brothers and sisters do you have?
   Eva: I have one brother and one sister.
   Fu-an: How old are they?
   Eva: My sister Rosie is 12 and my brother David is 22.
   Fu-an: Oh. And what do your parents do?
   Eva: My father is an engineer and my mother is a pharmacist.
   Fu-an: How old are they?
   Eva: My mother is 44 and my father is 45.

2. Ask this comprehension question:
   - *In general, what are the speakers talking about?* (family)

3. Say: *Listen again. This time listen to the details of the conversation.*

4. Play or read the conversation again, pausing for choral repetition. Allow students to write down the information as they listen. Play or read the conversation again, if needed, for students to get all the information.

5. Ask the following questions:
   - *How does Speaker 2 describe the size of her family?* (medium-sized)
   - *What is Speaker 1's first question?* (How many brothers and sisters do you have?)
   - *How many brothers and sisters does Speaker 2 have?* (one brother and one sister)
   - *What are their names?* (Rosie and David)
   - *How old are they?* (Rosie is 12 and David is 22.)
   - *What do Speaker 2's parents do?* (Her father is an engineer, and her mother is a pharmacist.)
   - *What is Speaker 1's last question?* (How old are they?)
   - *How old are Speaker 2's parents?* (Her mother is 44, and her father is 45.)

Elicit responses from various students.

PRONUNCIATION FOCUS

Class CD 1, Track 29

1. Explain what the focus is. Play or read the examples in the book and have students repeat chorally.

   How many brothers and sisters do you have?
   What do your parents do?
   How old are they?

2. With books open, play or read the conversation again. Tell students to pay attention to the intonation in the questions.

3. Paired Reading. Have students practice the conversation, switching roles.

22 Unit 3

Give It a Try

1. Talking about family members

Presentation

1. Have students look at the function box. Give them time to read the exchanges.

2. Model the exchanges and have students repeat chorally.

3. Practice a few exchanges with various students.

Note

Review question intonation. On the board, write the following questions and mark the intonation:

Do you have any brothers?

How many brothers do you have?

Model the questions and have students repeat.

Practice 1

Class CD 1, Track 30

1. Have students read the directions and look at the pictures.

2. Play or read the example conversation twice.

    A: Tell me about Sam's family.
    B: He comes from a medium-sized family.
    A: How many brothers and sisters does he have?
    B: He has two brothers.

3. Pair Work. Have students take turns asking and answering questions about the families in the pictures.

4. Have several pairs demonstrate their conversations for the class.

Practice 2

1. Have students read the directions for the activity and look at the chart.

2. Pair Work. Have students take turns asking and answering questions about each other's families and filling in the chart.

3. Have students report on their partner's family to the class.

Extension

Extend Practice 2 to find out: Who has the largest family? Who has the smallest family? Who has the most sisters? Who has the most cousins? Who has the greatest age difference between their oldest and youngest siblings? Who has the most family members living with them? Have students think of their own questions to ask about each other's families.

2. Asking about family members

Presentation

1. Have students look at the function box. Give them time to read the examples.

2. Model the exchanges and have students repeat chorally.

3. Practice a few exchanges with various students.

Note

Explain to students that in the United States there are several nicknames for family member terms. A mother is usually called *Mom* or *Mama*. A father is usually called *Dad* or *Pop*. A grandmother can be called *Grandma* or *Nana* and a grandfather *Grandpa* or *Papa*. There are also many variations of these. The terms *mother* and *father* are formal and are most often used to refer to someone else's parents.

Practice

Class CD 1, Track 31

1. Have students read the directions for the activity and look at the chart.

2. Play or read the example conversation twice.

    A: What do your parents do?
    B: My father is an engineer and my mother is a pharmacist.
    A: How old are they?
    B: My father is 44, and my mother is 42.
    A: What are their names?
    B: My dad's name is John, and my mother's name is Karen.

3. Give students time to fill in the chart with information about their own parents.

4. Pair Work. Have students take turns asking and answering questions about each other's parents.

5. Have students report about their partner's parents to the class.

Listen to This

Class CD 1, Track 32

Part 1

1. Have students read the directions and look at the choices.

2. Play the recording or read the conversation. Tell students to put a check next to the topics that are discussed in the conversation.

   F: So tell me about your family, Michelle.
   M: OK. Well, there are five people in my family. My mom is 42, and she has a small export business.
   F: That's interesting. What does she export?
   M: She exports furniture.
   F: I see.
   M: And I have one sister, Su-Jun. She's younger than me. She's 15. She's very good at music and plays the piano and the violin.
   F: How nice! And what about your dad? What does he do?
   M: He's a dentist. He's 44 and he studied in Canada.
   F: Really? And do you have any brothers?
   M: Yes, I have one older brother and one younger one. My older brother is 20, and my younger brother is 11. They're both crazy about soccer.
   F: And what about you? Are you too?
   M: No, not really.

3. Ask volunteers for the answers.

> **Answers:**
> family size, occupations, sports, music

Part 2

1. Have students read the directions and look at the chart.

2. Play or read the conversation again and tell students to write the information about Michelle's family.

3. Play the conversation again for students to check their answers, if necessary.

4. Ask volunteers for their answers.

> **Answers:**
> Brothers: 2; 20 and 11
> Sisters: 1; 15

Part 3

1. Have students read the directions and look at the chart.

2. Play or read the conversation again and tell students to write what Michelle's parents do.

3. Ask volunteers for their answers.

> **Answers:**
> mother: has a small export business
> father: dentist

Student Book pages 25 & 108

Person to Person

Part 1

1. Divide the class into pairs and have students decide who will be Student A and who will be Student B. Have Student B look at page 108.

2. Have students read the directions and look at their pictures.

3. To check comprehension, ask:
   Student A, What is one question you will ask your partner about Salina? (How old is Salina?) Give students who are Student A time to write the questions they will ask. Then ask:
   Student B, How will you answer Student A's question? (She is 22 years old.)

4. Pair Work. Have Student A ask Student B questions about the people in the pictures.

Part 2

1. Have students read the directions.

2. Pair Work. Have Student A tell Student B what they think Salina and Brendan do, and have student B respond.

Part 3

1. Have students read the directions and look at their pictures.

2. To check comprehension, ask:
   Student B, What is one question you will ask your partner about Pelisa? (How tall is she?) Give Students B time to write the questions they will ask. Then ask:
   Student A, How will you answer Student B's question? (She is 150 centimeters.)

3. Pair Work. Have Student B ask Student A questions about the people in the pictures.

Part 4

1. Have students read the directions.

2. Pair Work. Have Student B tell Student A what they think Pelisa and Trent do.

Now Try This

1. Have students read the directions.

2. Have students think of a celebrity to interview. Give them time to write questions. Circulate and help as needed.

3. Have volunteers read a few of their questions to the class. Have the class guess who they want to interview.

Extension

Divide the class into pairs and have students take turns being the celebrity their partner has chosen and interviewing each other.

Review: Units 1–3

Components

Student Book, pages 26–27
Class CD 1, Tracks 33–35

Student Book page 26

Listen to This Unit 1

Class CD 1, Track 33

Part 1

1. Have students read the directions and look at the statements.

2. Play or read the conversation.

> R: Who's that over there, Paul?
> P: Her name's Taylor.
> R: She's pretty.
> P: Yes, she is. She's my dance teacher.
> R: Oh, are you taking dance lessons, Paul?
> P: Yes, I am. Taylor's a very good dancer.
> R: Really? Is Taylor her last name?
> P: No, it's her first name. Her last name's Johnson.
> R: Nice name. Taylor Johnson.
> P: Yes, it is. Do you want to meet her?
> R: Sure!
> P: OK. [pause] Oh, Taylor, this is my friend Robert.
> T: Hello, Robert. Nice to meet you.
> R: Hi. Nice to meet you, too.

3. Have students check the correct column.

4. Play or read the conversation again for students to check their answers.

> **Answers:**
> 1. false
> 2. true
> 3. true
> 4. false
> 5. false

Part 2

1. Pair Work. Have students compare their answers.

2. Ask several students for their answers.

Give It a Try

Part 1

1. Have students read the directions and look at the two sets of phrases.

2. Give students time to match a phrase in the first column with a response from the second column.

3. Ask several students for their answers.

> **Answers:**
> 1. Hello.
> 2. Pretty good, thanks.
> 3. I'm Ricardo.
> 4. Nice to meet you, too.

Part 2

1. Pair Work. Have students practice the conversation with a partner.

2. Ask several students to demonstrate for the class.

Listen to This Unit 2

Class CD 1, Track 34

Part 1

1. Have students read the directions and look at the list of items and choices.

2. Play or read the conversation. Have students write the number of the item next to its location.

> A: Oh, no! I broke my glasses, and I can't see a thing without them.
> B: What are you looking for?
> A: Well, where's my bag? I thought I put it on the table last night.
> B: It's right there—in front of the table.
> A: OK. And it looks like it's going to rain. I'll need my umbrella when I go out. I usually put it under the table.
> B: No, it's not under the table. Look there, behind the table on the left. Do you see it?
> A: Oh, right. Thanks. And where did I put my notebook?
> B: Umm...I saw it somewhere a few minutes ago.
> A: Is it on the table?
> B: No. Let me look in the drawer. Yes, it's in here. And are you looking for your watch, too?
> A: Yes, I thought it was in the drawer, too.
> B: No, it isn't. It's on the table near the back.
> A: Oh, yeah. And I wonder where I put my cell phone.
> B: There it is. Under the table.
> A: How did it get there? Oh, and one more thing. Where's today's paper?
> B: There it is, on the floor next to the table.

3. Play or read the conversation again for students to check their answers.

4. Ask several students for the answers. Have a volunteer draw a picture on the board showing the table and the location of each item.

Answers:
1. It's in front of the table.
2. It's behind the table.
3. It's in the drawer.
4. It's on the table.
5. It's under the table.
6. It's next to the table.

Part 2

1. Have students read the directions.

2. Pair Work. Have students ask and answer questions about the locations of each item. Play or read the conversation again, if necessary.

Student Book page 27

Give It a Try

1. Have students read the directions and look at the pictures.

2. Pair Work. Have students take turns pointing to items and asking and answering *What's this?/What are these?*

3. Have several pairs demonstrate for the class.

Answers:
1. shoes
2. watch
3. purse
4. cap
5. ring
6. sneakers
7. jeans
8. jacket

Listen to This Unit 3

Class CD 1, Track 35

Part 1

1. Have students read the directions and look at the chart.

2. Play or read the conversation and have students check their answers in the chart.

M-J: What do you like to do in your free time, Rod?
R: Well, Min-joo, I'm into music, so I play guitar. I really love rock music. Do you like rock music?
M-J: Not really. I'm more interested in classical music. I play the piano and listen to a lot of piano music.
R: Are you interested in sports?

M-J: Not so much. But I love reading. I really like detective stories.
R: Oh, cool. How about you, Tina? Do you like music?
T: No, not really. I'm more into sports.
R: What kind of sports are you interested in?
T: I love tennis and basketball. And I also enjoy traveling. How about you, James? What are you interested in?
J: Actually, I really like traveling. I want to be a tour guide some day.
T: Really? Where do you like to travel?
J: Oh, everywhere, but I'm really interested in Asia—especially Thailand and Singapore.
T: OK. What else are you interested in? Do you like music?
J: Yes, I do. Especially rock.
M-J: So that leaves you, Kazu. What do you like to do in your free time?
K: Hmm. I guess traveling is something I love. I also like all kinds of sports. Especially surfing and swimming.

3. Play or read the conversation again for students to check their answers.

Answers:
Rod: rock music
Min-joo: classical music; reading
Tina: sports; traveling
James: traveling; rock music
Kazu: travel; sports

Part 2

1. Have students read the directions.

2. Pair Work. Have students discuss which people would enjoy spending time together.

Answers:
Tina and Kazu like sports, and traveling; Rod and James like rock music.

Give It a Try

Part 1

1. Have students read the directions and look at the chart.

2. Give students time to write what they like and dislike under each category.

3. Circulate and help as needed.

Part 2

1. Have students read the directions.

2. Pair Work. Have students take turns asking each other about the information in their chart.

Unit 4

What does she look like?

Components

Student Book, pages 28–35, 109
Class CD 1, Tracks 36–44
Optional Activities 4.1–4.2,
page 108

Objectives

Functions: Describing colors and clothing, describing people, giving opinions, talking about prices

Topics: Colors, clothing, physical characteristics, prices

Structures: *How much*, adjectives, colors, *What* questions

Pronunciation Focus: Difference in pronunciation of *fifty* and *fifteen*

Listen to This: Listening for names and relationships

Student Book page 28

CONSIDER THIS

1. Have students read the information and the question. Go over any vocabulary students don't know.

2. Group Work. Divide students into groups of four or five. Have students in each group take turns talking about questionnaires they have answered. Help students with vocabulary as needed.

3. Ask volunteers to share their experiences with the class.

Vocabulary

Introduce these words and phrases to the students:

Nice party: another way to say that you are having a good time at a party

nose ring: a small piece of jewelry worn on the nose

Prelistening

1. Pair Work. Have students open their books and look at the photograph. Have partners describe what they see to each other. Circulate and help with vocabulary as needed.

2. Class Work. Read the title of the conversation and the prelistening questions.

3. Pair Work. Have students ask and answer the questions about parties.

4. Ask volunteers to answer the questions.

Conversation 1

Class CD 1, Track 36

1. With books closed, play the recording or read the conversation.

   Tami: Hi, Joe. Nice party.
   Joe: Thanks, Tami.
   Tami: Sorry I'm late.
   Joe: That's OK. I'm glad you came.
   Tami: By the way, I'm looking for my sister. Is she here?
   Joe: What does she look like?
   Tami: She's tall, and she has long hair.
   Joe: Is she wearing a red dress?
   Tami: Yes, and she's wearing a nose ring.
   Joe: Oh, yes. She's in the kitchen.
   Tami: Thanks.

2. Ask these comprehension questions:

   • *Where are the speakers?* (a party)
   • *Is it Speaker 1's party?* (no)

3. Play or read the conversation again, pausing for choral repetition.

4. Ask the following questions:

   • *Is it Speaker 2's party? How do you know?* (Yes. He says "Thank you" to Speaker 1.)
   • *Is Speaker 1 on time?* (No, she was late.)
   • *Who is Speaker 1 looking for?* (her sister)
   • *What does she look like?* (tall with long hair)
   • *What is she wearing?* (a red dress and a nose ring)
   • *Where is she?* (in the kitchen)

   Elicit responses from various students.

5. Paired Reading. Have students read the conversation, switching roles.

Give It a Try

1. Describing colors and clothing

Presentation

1. Have students look at the function box. Give them time to read the examples.

2. Model the exchanges and have students repeat chorally.

3. Practice a few exchanges with various students. Encourage them to use colors from the art on the page or other colors they know in English.

Notes

1. English has words for many different shades of colors, and they are often used in everyday conversation when describing something. Some examples are *butter yellow, midnight blue, leaf green, chocolate brown*. *Dark, medium*, and *light* are often put in front of color words.

2. Review intonation of *What* questions. On the board, write:

What color are my shoes?

What color is the shirt?

Explain to students that the words that indicate the information that you want are the ones that are stressed. Ask students which words they think will be stressed in these sentences. Mark the stress. Model and have students repeat.

3. If time allows, teach other clothing vocabulary such as *sleeve, collar, button, belt, zipper, cuff*, etc. Encourage students to use these words when they are describing clothing.

Practice 1

Class CD 1, Track 37

1. Have students read the directions and look at the pictures. Go over any color and clothing vocabulary students don't know.

2. Play or read the example conversation twice.

   A: What colors are you wearing today?
   B: My shirt is red. My shoes are dark blue.

3. Give students time to write down four colors that they are wearing. Encourage them to be as descriptive as possible.

4. Pair Work. Have students take turns describing what they are wearing.

5. Have several pairs demonstrate for the class.

Practice 2

1. Have students read the directions and look at the example.

2. Pair Work. Have students take turns asking and answering questions about the color of other classmates' clothes.

3. Ask several volunteers to demonstrate for the class.

Practice 3

1. Have students read the directions and look at the example and the words in the word box.

2. Pair Work. Have students take turns saying a color and finding someone in the class wearing that color. Encourage students to use specific color words.

3. Have several pairs demonstrate for the class.

Extension

Bring in clothing catalogs. Have students look through them and note the color words used to describe the clothing. Alternatively, cover the color words and write them on the board. Have students guess which color word describes which article of clothing.

2. Describing people

Review. Have volunteers describe their own clothing or a classmate's clothing.

Presentation

1. Have students look at the function box. Give them time to read the examples.

2. Model the exchanges and have students repeat chorally.

3. Practice a few exchanges with various students.

Note

Explain to students that the phrase *look like* is only used when describing how something is perceived with the eyes. It is not to be confused with *sounds like, feels like, tastes like* which are used when describing how something is perceived with the ears, hands, and mouth.

Practice 1

Class CD 1, Track 38

1. Have students read the directions and look at the picture.

2. Play or read the example conversation twice.

   A: What does Sandy look like?
   B: She's medium height. She's wearing brown pants and a red shirt.

3. Pair Work. Have students take turns asking and answering questions about what the people in the picture look like and what they are wearing.

4. Ask several pairs to demonstrate for the class.

Practice 2

1. Have students read the directions and the example conversation. Give them time to think of how to describe another student in the class.

2. Pair Work. Have students take turns describing someone and guessing who is being described.

3. Ask several volunteers to demonstrate for the class.

Extension

Have students describe their family members to a partner. Have that student then show several pictures of different family members. Their partner then tries to guess who was described.

Listen to This

Class CD 1, Track 39

Part 1

1. Have students read the directions for the activity and look at the choices. To check understanding of the choices, ask students to name some examples of each (e.g. sports, movies, and gardening are *interests*; shy, friendly, and outgoing are *personality*)

2. Play the recording or read the descriptions. Tell students to check the qualities mentioned.

   1. He is medium height. He has curly hair and wears glasses. He likes bright colors.
   2. She's pretty short. She likes to wear her hair short. She wears glasses and today she's wearing pants. She and Anne are best friends.
   3. She's very tall. She has long blond hair and she's wearing a jacket and pants today. She is Ted's sister.
   4. He has long hair and is medium height, I guess. He often wears shorts and a cap.
   5. He's medium height, and a little heavy. He has short blond hair and likes to wear T-shirts and jeans. He is Bill's brother.

3. Play or read the conversation again for students to check their answers.

4. Ask volunteers for their answers.

> **Answers:**
> height, weight, hair, glasses, clothing

Part 2

1. Have students read the directions and look at the people.

2. Ask volunteers to describe each of the people.

3. Play or read the descriptions again. Have students write the number of the description next to the person described.

4. Play or read the conversation again for students to check their answers.

5. Ask volunteers for their answers.

> **Answers:**
> 1. Ted
> 2. Jolene
> 3. Anne
> 4. Bill
> 5. Ken

Part 3

1. Have students read the directions. Play or read the conversations again, if necessary.

2. Have students listen for the relationships and write down which people are best friends, brothers, and brother and sister.

3. Ask volunteers for their answers.

> **Answers:**
> 1. Jolene and Anne
> 2. Bill and Ken
> 3. Anne and Ted

Let's Talk

Part 1

1. Have students read the directions and look at the chart. Help with vocabulary as needed.

2. Give students time to fill out the chart with their own information.

3. Circulate and help as needed.

Part 2

1. Have students read the directions and look at the example conversation.

2. Pair Work. Have students take turns asking each other questions and filling in the second column.

3. Have students report on their partner's answers.

Extension

Class Discussion. Have students discuss how their clothing has changed over time. Have them talk about what they liked to wear when they were younger and how it is different from what they wear now.

Do you like this sweater?

Vocabulary

Introduce these words and phrases to the students:

not bad: informal phrase meaning good, but not great

try on: to put on a piece of clothing to see if it is the right size and looks good

certainly: a formal way to say *yes* in response to a question

changing room: a small room in a clothing store in which you can try on clothes

Prelistening

1. Have students open their books and look at the photograph. Ask:

   - *Where are the speakers?* (in a clothing store)
   - *What do you think they are talking about?* (if they like the sweater they are holding or not)

2. Pair Work. Read the title of the conversation and the prelistening questions. Have students take turns asking and answering the questions.

3. Class Work. Have pairs share their answers with the class.

Conversation 2

Class CD 1, Track 40

1. With books closed, play the recording or read the conversation.

   Joe: How do you like this sweater?
   Ana: Hmm…I don't like it very much. I don't like the color.
   Joe: OK. Well, how about this one?
   Ana: Yes, it's great. How much is it?
   Joe: It's 15 dollars.
   Ana: Fifty dollars!
   Joe: No, 15.
   Ana: Fifteen. That's not bad.
   Joe: Excuse me, please. I'd like to try this on.
   Clerk: Certainly. The changing room is over there.
   Joe: Thank you.

2. Ask these comprehension questions:

   - *What is the relationship between the first two speakers?* (friends)
   - *Who is the other person?* (the store clerk)

3. Say: *Listen again. This time listen to the details of the conversation.*

4. Play or read the conversation again, pausing for choral repetition. Allow students to write down the information as they listen. Play or read the conversation again, if needed, for students to get all the information.

5. Ask the following questions:

   - *Does Speaker 2 like the sweater? Why or why not?* (No. She doesn't like the color.)
   - *Does Speaker 2 like the second sweater?* (yes)
   - *How much is the sweater?* ($15)
   - *Why is Speaker 2 surprised?* (She thinks it is 50 dollars.)
   - *Does Speaker 2 think $15 is a good price?* (yes)
   - *What does Speaker 1 do next?* (tries it on in the changing room)

   Elicit responses from various students.

PRONUNCIATION FOCUS

Class CD 1, Track 41

1. Explain what the focus is. Play or read the examples in the book and have students repeat chorally.

thirteen	thirty
fourteen	forty
fifteen	fifty

2. Drill number pairs. Say several of the focus words in natural speed and have students write what they hear.

3. Paired Reading. Have students practice the conversation, switching roles.

Give It a Try

1. Giving opinions

Presentation

1. Have students look at the function box. Give them time to read the examples.

2. Model the exchanges and have students repeat chorally.

3. Practice a few exchanges with various students.

Practice 1

Class CD 1, Track 42

1. Have students read the directions and look at the pictures of the clothing items.

2. To check comprehension, ask several volunteers: *Do you like the shoes? What number will you write next to the picture?* Give students time to write their numbers next to each picture.

3. Play or read the example conversation twice.

   A: How do you like these shoes?
   B: They're great.

4. Pair Work. Have students take turns asking and answering questions about each clothing item.

5. Have several pairs report their answers to the class.

Practice 2

1. Have students read the directions and look at the words in the box.

2. Pair Work. Have students take turns telling each other about clothing they own and what they like about it.

3. Have volunteers share their partner's information with the class.

Extension

Bring in fashion magazines and have students choose an outfit that they like and one that they don't like. Have them describe the outfits and say why they like them and don't like them.

2. Talking about prices

Presentation

1. Have students look at the function box. Give them time to read the examples.

2. Model the exchanges and have students repeat chorally.

3. Practice a few exchanges with various students.

Notes

1. On the board, write the following statements and mark the intonation:

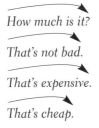

How much is it?

That's not bad.

That's expensive.

That's cheap.

Explain that adjectives are usually pronounced in such a way that the listener knows how the speaker feels. Model different ways of saying the responses above (surprised, angry, happy, etc.).

2. Explain that *It's OK* is another way to say *It's not bad.*

Practice

Class CD 1, Track 43

1. Have students read the directions and look at the pictures. Give students time to write how much they think each item costs.

2. Play or read the example conversation twice.

   A: How much is the watch?
   B: It's $55.00.
   A: That's not bad.

3. Pair Work. Have students compare their answers and react to their partner's prices.

4. Have students report their partner's prices and their reactions to the class.

Listen to This

Class CD 1, Track 44

Part 1

1. Have students read the directions and look at the chart.

2. To check comprehension, ask: *Which rows will you look at for this activity?* (the first three under the pictures)

3. Play or read the conversations. Tell students to check the correct row for each conversation depending on whether the speakers like the item a lot, think it's OK, or don't like it.

1

D: How do you like this phone?
J: Hmm. I like it a lot. It's very small, isn't it? And it's very light, too.
D: The screen is really sharp.
J: I'd love to get one. But how much is it?
D: It's $350.00.
J: Oh, that's too much for me. Let's try to find a cheaper one.

2

D: Hey, look at these shoes. What do you think of them?
J: I don't really like them. I don't like the design.
D: Yeah. They don't really look very nice. And look at the price—$199.00—way too expensive!
J: Yeah.

3

J: Are you looking for a new watch? Take a look at this one. What do you think?
D: It's not bad.
J: Yeah, it looks OK. But the price is really good. It's only $20.00.
D: That's cheap. I think I'll get it. I really need a new one.

4

J: Why don't you try on these sunglasses? I think they're really cool.
D: Let me see. Yeah...very cool!
J: And they're on sale. They're only $29.95.
D: That's not bad. I'll buy them. They'll be great for the beach.

4. Ask volunteers for the answers.

Answers:
1. like it a lot
2. don't like them
3. think it's OK
4. like them a lot

Part 2

1. Have students read the directions for the activity.

2. To check comprehension, ask: *Which row will you look at for this activity?* (the second to the last one)

3. Play or read the conversations again and tell students to listen for the price of each item.

4. Play or read the conversations again for students to check their answers.

5. Ask volunteers for their answers.

Answers:
| 1. $350 | 2. $199 |
| 3. $20 | 4. $29.95 |

Part 3

1. Have students read the directions.

2. To check comprehension, ask: *Which row will you look at for this activity?* (the last one)

3. Play or read the conversations again and tell students to listen to whether or not each person bought the items.

4. Ask volunteers for their answers.

Answers:
| 1. no | 2. no |
| 3. yes | 4. yes |

Extension

Class Discussion. Discuss prices of things. Ask the class what they think is a good price for everyday items, such as watches, TVs, a meal at a restaurant, etc.

Person to Person

Part 1

1. Divide the class into pairs and have students decide who will be Student A and who will be Student B. Have Student B look at page 109.

2. Have students read the directions and look at their pictures.

3. Give Students A time to make notes about what their "friend" looks like and what he is wearing. Give Students B time to look at the picture of the people and think how they would be described.

4. Circulate and help as needed.

Part 2

1. Have students read the directions.

2. Pair Work. Have Student A describe their "friend" to Student B. Student B says where the person is. (e.g. "He's the second person from the left, in the back of the room, talking with the guy in the purple top and dark pants.")

3. Have several pairs role-play for the class.

Part 3

1. Have students read the directions.

2. Give Students B time to make notes about what their "friend" looks like and what she is wearing. Give Students A time to look at the picture of the people and think how they would be described.

3. Pair Work. Have Students B describe their "friend" to Student A. Students A says where the person is. ("She's the second person from the right, in the back of the room, talking with the blond guy in the green shirt.")

4. Have several pairs role-play for the class.

Now Try This

1. Have students read the directions.

2. Group Work. Divide the class into groups of four. Have students describe unusual clothing they have seen.

3. Have a volunteer from each group tell the class about the most unusual clothing the group discussed.

What time is it?

Components

Student Book, pages 36–43
Class CD 1, Tracks 45–54
Optional Activities 5.1–5.2,
pages 108–109

Objectives

Functions: Telling the time, talking about routines, talking about the week, talking about activities

Topics: Time, daily schedules, everyday activities

Structures: *What time is it? Wh-* questions

Pronunciation Focus: Stress in questions

Listen to This: Listening to someone's schedule

Student Book page 36

CONSIDER THIS

1. Have students read the information and the questions. Go over any vocabulary students don't know.

2. Group Work. Divide students into groups of four or five. Have students in each group take turns asking and answering the questions. Help students with vocabulary as needed.

3. Ask volunteers to give their answers to the questions.

Vocabulary

Introduce these words and phrases to the students:

calling: contacting by telephone

night owl: a person who typically likes to go to bed very late

Prelistening

1. Pair Work. Have students open their books and look at the photograph. Have partners describe what they see to each other. Circulate and help with vocabulary as needed.

2. Class Work. Read the title of the conversation and the prelistening questions. Ask volunteers to answer the questions.

3. Class Work. Have the "night owls" go to one side of the room and the "early birds" go to the other side. Tell the groups to find out who is the earliest "early bird" and who is the latest "night owl." Have them report to the class.

Conversation 1

Class CD 1, Track 45

1. With books closed, play the recording or read the conversation.

   Jade: Who are you calling?
   David: I'm calling my sister in Sydney, Australia.
   Jade: What time is it there?
   David: I'm not sure.
   Jade: Well, it's 2 P.M. here, so it's about 12 A.M. there. That's very late.
   David: No problem. My sister always goes to bed late.
   Jade: Really. What time does she go to bed?
   David: Around 2 A.M. She's a real night owl!

2. Ask these comprehension questions:

   • *What is Speaker 2 doing?* (calling his sister)
   • *Is it morning, afternoon, or night?* (afternoon)

3. Play or read the conversation again, pausing for choral repetition.

4. Ask the following questions:

- *Where is Speaker 2's sister?* (Sydney, Australia)
- *Does he know what time it is in Australia?* (no)
- *What time is it where the speakers are?* (2 P.M.)
- *What time is it in Australia? What is the time difference?* (12 A.M., 10 hours)
- *What time does Speaker 2's sister go to bed?* (2 A.M.)

Elicit responses from various students.

5. Paired Reading. Have students read the conversation, switching roles.

Student Book page 37

Give It a Try

1. Telling the time

Presentation

1. Have students look at the function box. Give them time to read the examples.

2. Model the exchanges and have students repeat chorally.

3. Practice a few exchanges with various students.

Notes

1. Explain to students that P.M. is an abbreviation of *post meridiem* and A.M. is an abbreviation for *ante meridiem*. A.M. is used for the 12 hours from midnight to 11:00 in the morning; P.M. is used for the 12 hours from noon to 11:00 at night. In the United States, military time is seldom used (22:00, 13:00).

2. Explain that another way to say *ten-thirty* is *half past ten*.

3. Talk to students about punctuality in their culture and in the United States. Explain that being on time is generally very important in the United States. If someone is having a party and they specify a beginning time, it is very important to arrive close to that time. However, it is not good to arrive early. If it is a dinner party, it is important to arrive right on time. Discuss if that is the same or different in the students' cultures.

4. Tell students that to avoid confusion it is common to say *midnight* and *noon* instead of *12 A.M.* and *12 P.M.*

Practice 1

Class CD 1, Track 46

1. Have students read the directions and look at the clocks.

2. Play or read the example twice.

   A: It's 10:00.
   B: It's 10:05.

3. Pair Work. Have pairs take turns saying the times on the clocks. Encourage students to say each time more than one way (three-fifteen/quarter after three). Circulate and help as needed.

4. Ask volunteers for the answers.

Practice 2

Class CD 1, Track 47

1. Have students read the directions and look at the watches.

2. Play or read the example conversation twice.

   A: What time is it?
   B: It's 8:30.

3. Pair Work. Have students take turns asking and answering questions about the times on the clocks. Encourage students to say each time more than one way (ten to three/two-fifty).

Practice 3

1. Have students read the directions and look at the clocks and the example.

2. Pair Work. Have students take turns asking and answering questions about the time in different cities.

3. Have several pairs demonstrate for the class.

Extension

Class Discussion. Ask students if they have ever traveled to a different time zone and how they felt.

2. Talking about routines

Review. Say a time (three-thirty-five) and have a student say the time in a different way (twenty-five to three). Or, draw a clock face without hands on the board. Say a time and have a student come to the board and draw the time.

Presentation

1. Have students look at the function box. Give them time to read the examples.

2. Model the exchanges and have students repeat chorally.

3. Practice a few exchanges with various students.

Notes

1. Explain that another way to say *get up* is *wake up*. Another way to say *go to bed* is *go to sleep*. For the evening meal, some people say *supper* and some say *dinner*.

2. In English, it is correct to say *in the morning, in the afternoon,* and *in the evening,* but incorrect to say *in the night.* Instead say *at night* (I watch TV at night. I study in the morning).

Practice 1

Class CD 1, Track 48

1. Have students read the directions and look at the pictures and labels. Go over any vocabulary they don't know.

2. Play or read the example conversation twice.

   A: What time do you get up?
   B: I usually get up at 6:30. What time do you get up?

3. To check comprehension, ask a few students: *What time do you get up?*

4. Pair Work. Have students take turns asking and answering questions about what time they do the activities in the pictures. Encourage them to explain why they do each thing at that time. ("I have to get up at 6:00 because my bus comes at 7:00.")

5. Have students report on their partner's schedule.

Practice 2

1. Have students read the directions and look at the example.

2. Group Work. Divide the class into groups of four. Have students compare their routines.

3. Have a student from each group report on their group's schedules.

Extension

Divide the class into groups of three or four. Have them discuss how their daily schedules are different now than from what they were when they were younger. Also have them discuss how their schedules are different on different days of the week.

Listen to This

Class CD 1, Track 49

Part 1

1. Have students read the directions and look at the choices.

2. Play or read the conversation. Tell students to listen only for whether the people like their work or not, and write *yes* or *no* next to each name.

1
I: So you're a hair stylist, Chris?
C: That's right.
I: What's your job like?
C: It's great. I meet all kinds of interesting people. Last week an actor from that new TV soap opera came in for a cut.
I: Is that right? And do you work long hours?
C: Lots of my clients are working people, and they like to come in after work. So I start at 2:00 in the afternoon and finish at 10:00 at night.

2
I: So, Kayla, what does a dog walker do exactly?
K: I walk dogs, of course! I go to people's apartments, pick up their dogs, and take them for a walk. I walk six dogs at a time and walk them for two or three hours. Then I take them back and pick up another group of dogs and take them for a walk, too. Usually I start around 9:00 A.M. and finish at 4:00 in the afternoon.
I: And how do you like it?
K: I love it. I love dogs, and I love working outdoors so it's perfect for me.

3
I: Where are you working at the moment, Tim?
T: I'm working at the ticket office at the Verona Cinema.
I: Oh, yeah?
T: But I want to change jobs. The work is boring, the hours are really long, and the money isn't good.
I: What hours do you work?
T: I start at 10:30 A.M. We show the first movie of the day at 11:00. Then we often have late movies, and I have to be there until pretty late—usually until midnight.
I: Wow! That's a long day. No wonder you're looking for a new job.

4

I: What do you do, Celia?

C: I teach ballet.

I: That's interesting.

C: Yeah, I have my own studio. I don't dance professionally much anymore, so it's nice to be teaching ballet. I love it, and I have some great students.

I: Do you teach every day?

C: Not on Sunday, but I teach every other day. Most of my students come after school so I start at 3:00 in the afternoon. My last class is at 8:00 P.M. and I finish at 10:00. I'm really tired at the end of the day.

I: Yeah, I'm sure you are.

3. Play or read the conversation again for students to check their answers.

4. Ask volunteers for their answers.

Answers:

1. yes   2. yes   3. no   4. yes

Part 2

1. Have students read the directions and look at the job titles. Go over any vocabulary students don't know.

2. Play or read the conversations again and tell students to listen for what time each person starts their job and what time they finish.

3. Play or read the conversation again for students to check their answers.

4. Pair Work. Have students compare their answers.

5. Ask volunteers for their answers.

Answers:

hair stylist: 2:00–10:00 P.M.
dog walker: 9:00 A.M.–4:00 P.M.
ticket seller: 10:30–12:00 A.M. (midnight)
ballet teacher: 3:00–10:00 P.M.

Part 3

1. Have students read the directions.

2. Group Work. Divide the class into groups of three or four. Give them time to discuss the questions.

3. Have one person from each group report on their group's discussion.

Let's Talk

Part 1

1. Have students read the directions and look at the schedule book.

2. Have students write what they will do this weekend. Encourage students to make up funny and/or interesting things if they want to.

3. Circulate and help as needed.

Part 2

1. Have students read the directions and look at the sample questions and the words in the box. Brainstorm other possible weekend activities as a class.

2. Pair Work. Have students take turns asking and answering questions about each other's schedules.

3. Ask several pairs to demonstrate their conversation for the class.

Extension

Have students write their ideal daily schedule and explain it to the class.

Are you busy?

Vocabulary

Introduce these words and phrases to the students:

semester: a period of school usually lasting three or four months

so-so: not good, but not bad either

in really good shape: very healthy and physically fit

Prelistening

1. Have students open their books and look at the photograph. Ask students:

   - *Where are they?* (in a building on a college campus)
   - *What do you think they are talking about?* (their schedules)

2. Pair Work. Read the title of the conversation and the prelistening questions. Have students take turns asking and answering the questions.

3. Class Work. Have pairs share their answers with the class.

Conversation 2

Class CD 1, Track 50

1. With books closed, play the recording or read the conversation.

   Jade: Are you very busy this semester?
   Wei-de: So-so.
   Jade: What days do you have classes?
   Wei-de: I have classes on Tuesday, Wednesday, and Friday.
   Jade: And what do you do in your free time?
   Wei-de: Well, I go to the gym on Monday and Thursday. And I play tennis on Saturday afternoon.
   Jade: Wow! You must be in really good shape! And what do you do on Sunday?
   Wei-de: On Sunday I sleep until noon!

2. Ask this comprehension question:

   - *In general, what are the speakers talking about?* (Speaker 2's schedule)

3. Say: *Listen again. This time listen to the details of the conversation.*

4. Play or read the conversation again, pausing for choral repetition. Allow students to write down the information as they listen. Play or read the conversation again, if needed, for students to get all the information.

5. Ask the following questions:

   - *Is Speaker 2 busy?* (not too busy)
   - *What days does Speaker 2 have classes?* (Tuesday, Wednesday, and Friday)
   - *Does Speaker 2 play any sports?* (yes)
   - *What does Speaker 2 do on Monday and Thursday?* (goes to the gym)
   - *What does Speaker 2 do on Saturday?* (plays tennis)
   - *Does Speaker 2 play tennis in the morning?* (no, in the afternoon)
   - *What does Speaker 2 do on Sunday?* (sleeps until noon)

   Elicit responses from various students.

PRONUNCIATION FOCUS

Class CD 1, Track 51

1. Explain what the focus is. On the board, write the example questions. Play or read the examples in the book and have students repeat chorally, noticing which words are stressed.

   What days do you have classes?
   What do you do on Sunday?

2. With books open, play or read the conversation again. Tell students to pay attention to the stressed words in the questions.

3. Paired Reading. Have students practice the conversation, switching roles.

Give It a Try

1. Talking about the week

Presentation

1. Have students look at the function box. Give them time to read the words.

2. Model the pronunciation of the days of the week and have students repeat chorally.

Note

Explain that in the United States there is a traditional separation between the school/work week and the weekend. Discuss if this is the same in the students' cultures.

Practice 1

Class CD 1, Track 52

1. Have students read the directions.

2. Play or read the days of the week twice.

Monday
Tuesday
Wednesday
Thursday
Friday
Saturday
Sunday

3. Pair Work. Have students take turns saying the days of the week. If this is easy, have them see who can say all the days of the week the fastest.

Practice 2

1. Have students read the directions and look at the chart and the example. Give students time to check when they usually do each activity.

2. Pair Work. Have students take turns asking and answering questions about when they do the various activities.

3. Have several pairs demonstrate their conversations for the class.

Practice 3

1. Have students read the directions and look at the example. Have them think of two additional things they do on weekdays and on the weekend.

2. Pair Work. Have students take turns telling each other about the other things they do.

3. Have students report on their partner's activities.

2. Talking about activities

Presentation

1. Have students look at the function box. Give them time to read the examples.

2. Model the exchanges and have students repeat chorally.

3. Practice a few exchanges with various students.

Notes

1. Remind students that stress is given to the content words in a sentence. Content words are the nouns, verbs, adjectives, and adverbs. These words are said louder and held longer. Other parts of a sentence, auxiliary verbs, articles, pronouns, and prepositions are usually not stressed. On the board write the following sentences:

   What days do you have classes?

   Do you have classes on Friday?

   I go to a club.

   Have volunteers go to the board and mark the content words in each sentence. Model the sentences and have students repeat.

2. Review intonation of *Yes, I do* and *No, I don't*. Write the responses on the board and mark the intonation. Model the intonation and have students repeat.

Practice 1

1. Have students read the directions and look at the chart.

2. Give students time to fill in the chart with one activity they do each day of the week.

3. Circulate and help as needed.

Practice 2

Class CD 1, Track 53

1. Have students read the directions.

2. Play or read the example conversation twice.

   A: Do you have classes on Friday?
   B: No, I don't.
   A: What do you do on Friday nights?
   B: I go out with my friends.

3. Pair Work. Have students take turns asking and answering questions about each other's week.

4. Have several pairs demonstrate their conversations to the class.

Listen to This

Class CD 1, Track 54

Part 1

1. Have students read the directions. Make sure they understand what *get together* means.

2. Play or read the conversation.

   H: Are you busy this week, Paul? When can we get together to see a movie or something?
   P: Let me check. OK. So I'm going ice-skating with Kelly on Monday at 4:00 P.M. I guess we'll be there until dinnertime and then go off together. So Monday's not good. On Tuesday I have a guitar lesson at 5:00 P.M. It only lasts an hour so I'm free after that.
   H: Tuesday's not good for me. I have a Spanish class that starts at 6:00.
   P: Thursday I need to make an appointment to see the doctor. And Suzie's birthday party is on Friday night at 8:00 so Friday's not good for me.
   H: How about Saturday?
   P: Hmm...I'm not sure about Saturday. I want to see the dentist, and I want to make an appointment some time on Saturday morning. And Saturday afternoon, I'm meeting Terry and Pat for coffee at 2:30.
   H: OK. So it looks like Wednesday night is good for you?
   P: Sure. Wednesday looks good.

3. Ask volunteers for the answers.

   Answer:
   Wednesday night

Part 2

1. Have students read the directions and look at the chart.

2. Play or read the conversation again. Tell students to write the day of the week and the time Paul is going to do each activity.

3. Play the conversation again for students to check their answers.

4. Pair Work. Have students compare their answers.

5. Ask volunteers for their answers.

   Answers:
   ice-skating: Monday at 4:00
   guitar lesson: Tuesday at 5:00
   birthday party: Friday at 8:00
   meet for coffee: Saturday at 2:30

Part 3

1. Have students read the directions.

2. Play or read the conversation again and tell students to listen for who is busier, Paul or Hannah.

3. Ask volunteers for their answers.

   Answer:
   Paul

Extension

Divide the class into pairs. Have them write their own dialog about two people trying to find a time to get together. They should use the Listen to This dialog as a guide. Encourage students to use their imaginations and think of interesting, funny, or outrageous activities. Then have pairs perform their role play for the class.

Person to Person

Part 1

1. Have students read the instructions and look at the chart.

2. Give students time to fill in the first column of the chart.

Part 2

1. Have students read the directions.

2. Pair Work. Have students take turns asking and answering questions about each other's activities and have them fill in the second column in the chart.

3. Pair Work. Have students compare their answers and discuss how similar or different their schedules are.

4. Have pairs report their discussions to the class.

Now Try This

1. Have students read the directions.

2. Pair Work. Have students work in pairs to guess another classmate's answers to the questions in the chart.

3. Class Work. Have students walk around the class and ask the other student if their guesses were correct.

Extension

Have the class vote on who has the busiest schedule in the class, who has the most interesting schedule, and who has the easiest schedule.

Components

Student Book, pages 44–51
Class CD 1, Tracks 55–63
Optional Activities 6.1–6.2,
page 109

Objectives

Functions: Talking and giving an opinion about school, talking about and comparing personal qualities

Topics: Classes, studies, personal qualities

Structures: *How* and *What* questions

Pronunciation Focus: Syllable stress

Listen to This: Listening to someone else's opinions

Student Book page 44

CONSIDER THIS

1. Have students read the information and the question. Go over any vocabulary students don't know.

2. Group Work. Divide students into groups of four or five. Have students take turns talking about their experiences with Internet chat rooms. Help students with vocabulary as needed.

3. Ask volunteers to share their experiences with the class.

Vocabulary

Introduce these words and phrases to the students:

What do you do?: a common question to ask when you want to know what a person's occupation or main daily activity is

fashion design: the study of how to make and style clothing

awesome: wonderful; great

Prelistening

1. Pair Work. Have students open their books and look at the photograph. Have partners describe what they see to each other. Circulate and help with vocabulary as needed.

2. Class Work. Read the title of the conversation and the prelistening questions. Ask volunteers to answer the questions.

3. Pair Work. Have students take turns asking and answering the questions. Help with vocabulary as needed.

4. Class Work. Ask new volunteers to answer the questions. Make a list on the board of classes students like and dislike.

Conversation 1

Class CD 1, Track 55

1. With books closed, play the recording or read the conversation.

   Lisa: So what do you do, Emi?
   Emi: I'm a student. I'm studying fashion design.
   Lisa: That's interesting. And where are you studying?
   Emi: At City College.
   Lisa: How do you like your classes there?
   Emi: I love them. They're a lot of fun.
   Lisa: That's great.
   Emi: So what do you think of my top? It's my own design.
   Lisa: It's awesome!

2. Ask these comprehension questions:

   • *Do the speakers know each other well?* (no)
   • *How do you know?* (Speaker 1 doesn't know what Speaker 2 does.)

3. Play or read the conversation again, pausing for choral repetition.

4. Ask the following questions:

- *What does Speaker 2 do?* (She's a student.)
- *What is Speaker 2 studying?* (fashion design)
- *Where is Speaker 2 studying?* (City College)
- *What does Speaker 2 think of her classes?* (She loves them; they're fun.)
- *What does Speaker 1 think of Speaker 2's top?* (It's awesome!)

Elicit responses from various students.

5. Paired Reading. Have students read the conversation, switching roles.

Student Book page 45

Give It a Try

1. Talking about school

Presentation

1. Have students look at the function box. Give them time to read the examples.

2. Model the exchanges and have students repeat chorally.

3. Practice a few exchanges with various students.

Notes

1. Explain that a *major* is a person's main subject of study. Universities in the United States are usually four-year programs. During those four years, students are required to take classes in a variety of subjects, but they will major in one particular subject. The degree they receive at the end of those four years is in their major (a bachelor's degree in chemistry). After the first four years, a student can continue for an additional two years of study in their major and receive a master's degree, and then an additional 3–5 years for a Ph.D. Students can go to separate professional programs, such as law, business, or medicine, and receive special degrees in those studies

2. IT is an abbreviation for Information Technology. IT has become a popular and important major because companies rely on computers so much now.

3. Have several pairs demonstrate for the class.

Practice 1

Class CD 1, Track 56

1. Have students read the directions and look at the identification cards and questions. Go over any vocabulary students don't know.

2. Play or read the example conversation twice.

A: What does Emi do?
B: She's a college student.
A: Where is she studying?
B: She goes to City College.
A: What is she studying?
B: She's majoring in fashion design.

3. Pair Work. Have students take turns asking and answering questions about the people shown on the ID cards.

4. Ask volunteers to talk about each ID card.

Student Book page 46

Practice 2

1. Have students read the directions and look at the chart and the questions.

2. Give students time to fill out the chart with their own information.

3. Pair Work. Have students take turns asking and answering questions and recording their partner's information in the chart.

4. Have students report on their partner's answers.

Extension

Ask the class which classmate has the most interesting major. Ask them if they enjoy studying their major and, if not, what they would like to major in.

2. Giving an opinion about school and study

Review. Say the name of a popular movie or TV program. Go quickly around the classroom asking students their opinion of it using *How do you like…?*

Presentation

1. Have students look at the function box. Give them time to read the examples.

2. Model the exchanges and have students repeat chorally.

3. Practice a few exchanges with various students.

Note

Teach students other opinion responses such as *It's great! I don't like it so much, It's really good, It's not so bad, etc.*

Practice 1

Class CD 1, Track 57

1. Have students read the directions. Tell them to look at the faces, and the words and phrases in the Use These Words list. Review which responses would be appropriate for each face.

2. Have students look at the list. Give them time to think of their own ideas. Brainstorm ideas as a class, if necessary.

3. Play or read the example conversation twice.

   A: How do you like your school?
   B: It's OK.
   A: And how do you like your classes?
   B: I like them a lot.

4. Pair Work. Have pairs take turns asking and giving their opinions about the things on the list.

Practice 2

1. Have students read the directions and look at the chart and the example. Go over any vocabulary students don't know.

2. Give students time to check their responses in the chart. To check comprehension, ask a few students which column they will check for, e.g., How they like learning English by studying grammar or practicing dialogs, etc.

3. Pair Work. Have students take turns asking and answering questions about their responses in their chart.

4. Have students report on their partner's responses.

Extension

Ask students to explain how often they have tried each of the methods in the chart and why they think each method is effective or not.

Listen to This

Class CD 1, Track 58

Note

Explain that junior college is a two-year program. Liberal arts is a course of study that includes most or all of the humanities (literature, foreign language, arts, etc.) and social sciences (history, sociology, etc.).

Part 1

1. Have students read the directions.

2. Play or read the conversations. Tell students to listen for how each person feels about school.

   1
   I: Where are you going to school, Martin?
   M: I'm a freshman at City University.
   I: Uh-huh. I hear it's a very good university.
   M: Yes, it is. I'm really happy there.
   I: Are you studying fine arts?
   M: No, I am studying IT.
   I: I see. And how do you like your classes?
   M: They're OK. Some are kind of difficult, but the professors are really good.

   2
   I: Where are you studying, Rosie?
   R: I'm still at the local junior college. It's really boring. But I'm hoping to go to the university next semester.
   I: What are you studying?
   R: I'm doing a general liberal arts course.
   I: Do you have a major?
   R: Yes, I'm studying American literature. But it's not very interesting. I haven't learned anything new all year.

   3
   I: What are you studying, Liz?
   L: I'm majoring in music.
   I: Great. That must be very interesting.
   L: Yes, it is. I love it. And I have great teachers. Some of them are pretty famous musicians.
   I: Wonderful. And where are you studying?
   L: I'm at the national university. I love it!

3. Ask volunteers for their answers.

   Answer:
   Liz likes it the best; Rosie likes it the least.

Part 2

1. Have students read the directions and look at the chart. Go over any vocabulary students don't know.

2. Play or read the conversations again and tell students to listen for what kind of school each person is attending and what they are studying.

3. Play or read the conversations again for students to check their answers.

4. Ask volunteers for their answers.

> **Answers:**
> Martin: university; IT
> Rosie: junior college; Liberal Arts
> Liz: university; Music

Part 3

1. Have students read the directions and look at the chart.

2. Play or read the conversations again. Tell students to listen for how each person likes his/her school and major.

3. Ask volunteers for their answers.

> **Answers:**
> Martin: Like it a lot; So-so
> Rosie: Don't like; Don't like
> Liz: Like it a lot; Like it a lot

Part 4

1. Have students read the directions.

2. Play or read the conversations again, if necessary.

3. Pair Work. Have students talk about who will change their major and who will be the most successful.

4. Have students report on their discussions to the class.

Let's Talk

Part 1

1. Have students read the directions and look at the chart and the words in the box. Make sure students understand the opinion words in the directions, as well as the majors in the box.

2. Give students time to write their information in the chart.

3. Circulate and help as needed.

Part 2

1. Have students read the directions and look at the example conversation.

2. Pair Work. Have students take turns asking and answering questions about each other's charts.

3. Have students report on their partner's answers.

Extension

Have students write their ideal course of study and tell the class.

Tell me about your friend.

Student Book page 48

Vocabulary

Introduce these words and phrases to the students:

best friend: the friend with whom you have the closest relationship

outgoing: very friendly

talkative: talking a lot

easygoing: difficult to make angry or upset

reliable: able to be trusted with important things

Prelistening

1. Have students open their books and look at the photograph. Ask students:

   • *Where are the speakers?* (in class)
   • *How do you know?* (There is a whiteboard with a homework assignment and the speakers have notebooks and are sitting at desks.)

2. Pair Work. Read the title of the conversation and the prelistening questions. Have students take turns asking and answering the questions.

3. Class Work. Have pairs share their answers with the class.

Conversation 2

Class CD 1, Track 59

1. With books closed, play the recording or read the conversation.

   Ali: So, who is your best friend?
   Emi: I guess that's my friend Sara.
   Ali: Tell me about her. What's she like?
   Emi: Oh, she's great. She's very funny. And she's interesting to talk to.
   Ali: Really?
   Emi: Yes, she's very outgoing and talkative.
   Ali: And is she easygoing?
   Emi: Oh, sure. That's why I like her. The only thing is, she's forgetful at times. She's not very reliable.
   Ali: Yeah?
   Emi: Yes. We have an appointment, and she's late. That's Sara!

2. Ask this comprehension question:

   • *In general, what are the speakers talking about?* (Speaker 2's best friend)

3. Say: *Listen again. This time listen to the details of the conversation.*

4. Play or read the conversation again, pausing for choral repetition. Allow students to write down the information as they listen. Play or read the conversation again, if needed, for students to get all the information.

5. Ask the following questions:

   • *Who is Speaker 2's best friend?* (Sara)
   • *Does Speaker 2 enjoy talking to Sara? Why?* (yes; She's funny and interesting.)
   • *Is Sara shy and quiet?* (no; She's outgoing and talkative.)
   • *What is Sara's only bad quality?* (She's forgetful and not reliable.)

   Elicit responses from various students.

PRONUNCIATION FOCUS
Class CD 1, Track 60

1. Explain what the focus is. Write the column headings *1st Syllable* and *2nd Syllable* on the board. With books closed, model the examples in the book and have students repeat chorally.

2. Ask students to tell you in which column you should write each word.

1st syllable	2nd syllable
different	easygoing
talkative	reliable
interesting	forgetful

3. With books open, play or read the conversation again. Tell students to pay attention to which syllables are stressed.

4. Paired Reading. Have students practice the conversation, switching roles.

Give It a Try

1. Talking about personal qualities

Presentation

1. Have students look at the function box. Give them time to read the examples.

2. Model the exchanges and have students repeat chorally.

3. Practice a few exchanges with various students.

Notes

1. Make sure students do not confuse *What's she like?* with *What does she like?* The first one is asking about someone's personality, and the second is asking about someone's preferences.

2. Review the intonation of questions. On the board, write:

What's Sarah like?

Is she easygoing?

Mark the intonation and model the questions for the class. Have students practice, substituting different names and adjectives.

Practice 1

Class CD 1, Track 61

1. Have students read the directions for the activity and look at the words and the chart.

2. Play or read the example conversation twice.

   A: I think fun is a positive quality.
   B: I agree.
   A: I think talkative is a negative quality. What do you think?

3. Give students time to write the adjectives in the chart under the column where they think they belong. Make sure they understand that positive qualities are ones they think are good for people to have and negative ones are bad for people to have.

4. Pair Work. Have students discuss each other's charts. Have them make a separate list of adjectives that they disagree on.

5. Have pairs report on their discussion to the class. Have the class discuss the adjectives that pairs disagreed on.

Practice 2

1. Have students read the directions for the activity and look at the chart and the example.

2. Give students time to think of three adjectives that describe their friend.

3. Pair Work. Have students take turns talking about their friend.

4. Have several pairs demonstrate their conversations for the class.

Extension

Class Discussion. Discuss with students the most important and the least important qualities in a friend, a mother, a sibling, a teacher, etc. Write students' answers on the board. Have students vote on the single most important and the single least important quality for each person.

2. Comparing personal qualities

Presentation

1. Have students look at the function box. Give them time to read the examples.

2. Model the exchanges and have students repeat chorally.

3. Practice a few exchanges with various students.

Practice 1

Class CD 1, Track 62

1. Have students read the directions for the activity and look at the example and the words in the box.

2. Play or read the example conversation twice.

   A: Who is your best friend?
   B: My best friend is my sister, Anna.
   A: How similar are you?
   B: Well, we are both talkative.
   A: And how are you different?

3. Pair Work. Have students take turns comparing themselves to a friend or sibling.

Practice 2

1. Have students read the directions for the activity and look at the chart.

2. Give students time to think of a particular friend and fill in the chart with both their own and their friend's qualities.

3. Pair Work. Have students take turns asking and answering questions about each other's chart.

4. Have students report their discussion to the class by pointing out similarities and differences between themselves and their friend.

Listen to This

Class CD 1, Track 63

Part 1

1. Have students read the directions for the activity and look at the chart. Go over vocabulary as necessary.

2. Play or read the conversation twice. Tell students to check what Colin likes about his roommate.

   W: How is everything at college this year, Colin?
   C: Pretty good.
   W: Do you like the dormitory?
   C: Yes. My roommate is from Brazil.
   W: Oh, yeah. What's he like?
   C: Well, he's really friendly. He is always meeting new people. And he has a great sense of humor. He always makes me laugh.
   W: That's nice.

   C: Yeah. He's a very good student and studies very hard. And he's kind of interesting, too. He likes insects and is always coming back with some strange insect he found somewhere. And he has two big black spiders as pets. He keeps them in a big jar next to his bed.
   W: That sounds a little creepy.
   C: Oh, I don't mind. I wish he would keep his part of the room a little cleaner though. He leaves things on the floor all the time.
   W: Is that right?
   C: And he's pretty forgetful, too. Sometimes he says he wants to meet me for lunch in the cafeteria but half the time he forgets and never shows up.
   W: Oh, dear. That's too bad.

3. Ask volunteers for the answers.

   Answers:
   likes: friendly, interesting, funny, good student

Part 2

1. Have students read the directions for the activity and look at the chart.

2. Play or read the conversation again. Tell students to put an ✗ in the "dislikes" column for the things Colin doesn't like about his roommate.

   Answers:
   dislikes: untidy; forgetful

Part 3

1. Have students read the directions for the activity.

2. Give students time to write three qualities they think are important for a roommate.

3. Ask volunteers for their answers.

Extension

Ask students if they have a roommate now or if they have ever had a roommate. Have them describe their roommate to the class.

Person to Person

Part 1

1. Have students read the instructions and look at the questions and the chart.

2. Give students time to fill in the first four notepads.

3. Circulate and help as needed.

Part 2

1. Have students read the directions for the activity.

2. Pair Work. Have students take turns asking and answering questions about the information in their chart. Tell students to write their partner's information on the other four notepads.

Part 3

1. Have students read the directions for the activity. Place students in groups of four.

2. Group Work. Have students report their partner's answers to the group. Have the group discuss how similar they all are.

Now Try This

1. Have students read the directions.

2. Give students time to decide which field is best for them and why.

3. Pair Work. Have students compare each other's answers.

4. Class Work. Have the class compare their answers.

Extension

Extend the Now Try This discussion. Have students talk about which field they think would be perfect for their classmates.

Review:
Units 4–6

Components

Student Book, pages 52–53
Class CD 1, Tracks 64–66

Student Book page 52

Listen to This Unit 4

Class CD 1, Track 64

Part 1

1. Have students read the directions and look at the chart.

2. Play or read the conversation.

> B: Hi, Kim. I'm at immigration now. I won't be long.
> K: Great. I'm waiting in the meeting area.
> B: I don't know what you look like. How tall are you?
> K: Uh, well I'm pretty tall. Are you tall or short?
> B: I guess I'm medium height.
> K: And I have short brown hair. How about you?
> B: I have black hair.
> K: Are you wearing glasses?
> B: No, I'm not. Are you?
> K: Yes, I am.
> B: OK. And what are you wearing? I'm wearing brown pants and a blue shirt.
> K: I'm wearing blue jeans and a yellow top.
> B: Great. So I'll see you in a few minutes.
> K: Yeah. I'm sure I can find you.

3. Have students write the correct information about each person's appearance in the chart.

4. Play or read the conversation again for students to check their answers.

> **Answers:**
> Kim: tall; short brown hair; glasses; blue jeans; yellow top
> Bob: medium height; black hair; brown pants; blue shirt

Part 2

1. Pair Work. Have students take turns asking and answering questions to find out if they have the same information in their charts.

2. Ask several students to model their conversations for the class.

Give It a Try

Part 1

1. Have students read the directions and look at the two sisters in the picture.

2. Have students note differences between the sisters and list as many as they can.

Part 2

1. Pair Work. Have students take turns telling each other about all the similarities and differences they noticed. Find out who noticed the most differences.

2. Have several pairs demonstrate for the class.

Listen to This Unit 5

Class CD 1, Track 65

Part 1

1. Have students read the directions and look at the chart.

2. Play or read the conversation and have students write *A* when Anna is busy and *D* when Dave is busy.

> A: So why don't we try to meet for dinner some time this week?
> D: That would be great. But I have a pretty busy week. How about you?
> A: Me too. But let's see if we can find a day when we're both free.
> D: Well, I can't do it tonight. I have a math class until 9:00 P.M. on Mondays.
> A: Yuck. Anyway, I'm not free tonight either.
> D: That's too bad. Now let's see. How does Tuesday look for you? It's OK for me.
> A: Let me think. Oh, I can't do Tuesday. I have a driving lesson. And Wednesday night, my sister and I always go to the gym.
> D: Wednesday's not good for me either because I have a basketball game.
> A: Hey, this is getting difficult. What else have I got on this week? Oh, yes. I have a meeting I have to go to on Friday. The weekend I am not free at all because I promised to meet friends on both Saturday and Sunday.
> D: So where does that leave us? I don't have anything else planned for this week.

3. Play or read the conversation again for students to check their answers.

4. Ask several students for the answers.

> **Answers:**
> Anna: driving lesson Tuesday; go to the gym Wednesday; meeting Friday; meet friends Saturday and Sunday
> Dave: late class Monday; play basketball Wednesday

Part 2

1. Have students read the directions.

2. Pair Work. Have students figure out when Anna and Dave can meet. Play or read the conversation again, if necessary.

> **Answer:**
> Thursday

Student Book page 53

Give It a Try

1. Have students read the directions and look at the questions.

2. Pair Work. Have students take turns asking the questions and answering them.

3. Have several pairs demonstrate for the class.

Listen to This Unit 6

Class CD 1, Track 66

Part 1

1. Have students read the directions and look at the chart. Review the adjectives, if necessary.

2. Have students put an ✗ next to the qualities they think are important in a roommate and a travel companion.

3. Play or read the conversation and have students check the speakers' opinions.

> A: I think for a roommate, you want someone who is really considerate—someone who doesn't only think about themselves. They think about the other person, you know, so they don't have the TV on when the other person is sleeping, that kind of thing.
> B: Right. And I like someone who keeps the place clean—they don't leave their clothes all over the room and stuff like that.
> A: And it's also good if they know how to do things, like cooking, and fixing things that go wrong, or even if they know how to change a lightbulb.
> B: Yes. It's great if a roommate is practical. How about good qualities for a travel companion?
> A: Well, a travel companion should be practical, too. And you want someone to keep you company. They should be friendly and talkative.
> B: Right. And someone who likes meeting people and who is outgoing. Because it's nice to get to meet people when you're traveling. Otherwise, what's the point of leaving home?
> A: And if you're going to spend a lot of time together, you want someone who is easy to get along with. They don't lose their temper or get stressed out.
> B: Right. They should be relaxed and friendly.

4. Play or read the descriptions again for students to check their answers.

> **Answers:**
> Roommate: responsible; practical; considerate
> Travel companion: friendly; outgoing; easygoing; relaxed; talkative; practical

Part 2

1. Have students read the directions.

2. Pair Work. Have students compare the items they marked with an ✗ to the items they marked with a ✓ and discuss with their partner whether they agree with the speakers or not. Encourage them to give reasons for why they agree or disagree with the speakers.

Give It a Try

1. Have students read the directions and look at the chart and the adjectives. Brainstorm other adjectives if necessary.

2. Give students time to write three adjectives under each subject.

3. Group Work. Have students compare their answers.

4. Have one person from each group report on the group's discussion.

Unit 7 — I love tennis!

Components

Student Book, pages 54–61
Class CD 2, Tracks 2–12
Optional Activities 7.1–7.2,
page 110

Objectives

Functions: Talking about routines, asking about the weekend, talking about past events

Topics: Weekend activities, past events

Structures: *Do you ever…?* adverbs of time, past tense

Pronunciation Focus: Pronunciation of *was*

Listen to This: Listening to someone's activities

Student Book page 54

CONSIDER THIS

1. Have students read the information and the questions. Go over any vocabulary students don't know.

2. Group Work. Divide students into groups of four or five. Have students in each group take turns asking and answering the questions. Help students with vocabulary as needed.

3. Have students talk about their activities.

Vocabulary

Introduce these words and phrases to the students:

go for a run: to exercise by running outdoors for a period of time

brunch: a meal that is later than breakfast but earlier than lunch usually eaten on Saturday or Sunday

Why don't we (play tennis)?: Let's (play tennis).

Prelistening

1. Pair Work. Have students open their books and look at the photograph. Have partners describe what they see to each other. Circulate and help with vocabulary as needed.

2. Class Work. Read the title of the conversation and the prelistening questions. Ask volunteers to answer the questions.

3. Pair Work. Have students take turns asking and answering the questions. Help with vocabulary as needed.

4. Class Work. Ask new volunteers to answer the questions. Make a list on the board of students' favorite things to do on weekends.

Conversation 1

Class CD 2, Track 2

1. With books closed, play the recording or read the conversation.

   Mei-ho: What do you usually do on Saturday?
   Tasha: I usually get up early and go for a run in the morning. Then I meet my friends and we have brunch together.
   Mei-ho: What about in the afternoon?
   Tasha: In the afternoon I often see a movie or go over to my friend's house.
   Mei-ho: And do you ever play sports on the weekend?
   Tasha: Yeah, sometimes I play tennis.
   Mei-ho: I love tennis. Why don't we play together sometime?
   Tasha: Sure. That sounds great.

2. Ask this comprehension question:

   • *In general, what are the speakers talking about?* (Speaker 2's weekend activities)

3. Play or read the conversation again, pausing for choral repetition.

4. Ask the following questions:
   - *What day are the speakers talking about?* (Saturday)
   - *What does Speaker 2 do in the morning?* (go for a run and meet friends for brunch)
   - *What does Speaker 2 do in the afternoon?* (see a movie or go to a friend's house)
   - *What else does Speaker 2 on the weekend?* (plays tennis)
   - *What does Speaker 1 ask Speaker 2 to do? Why?* (to play tennis; She loves tennis.)

   Elicit responses from various students.

5. Paired Reading. Have students read the conversation, switching roles.

Student Book page 55

Give It a Try

1. Talking about routines (1)

Presentation

1. Have students look at the function box. Give them time to read the examples.

2. Model the exchanges and have students repeat chorally.

3. Practice by having various students respond with their own information.

Notes

1. Review pronunciation and intonation. On the board, write:

   What do you usually do on Saturday morning?

   First practice the pronunciation of the first part of the question *What do you usually do*. Model the pronunciation and have students repeat several times. Have students try to say it as fast as they can three times in a row. Then, mark the intonation of the sentence. Point out that the content words *Saturday morning* are stressed. Model the whole question and have students repeat. Have students practice the question several times, substituting different pronouns, days, and times of day.

2. Explain that *surf the web* means to browse different web sites on the Internet. *Hang out* means to spend time with someone without doing anything specific.

Practice 1

Class CD 2, Track 3

1. Have students read the directions and look at the chart.

2. Play or read the example conversation twice.

   A: What do you usually do on Saturday morning?
   B: I usually surf the web and sometimes I play sports. What about you?
   A: Saturday morning? I always sleep in!

3. Give students time to mark their answers on the chart.

4. Pair Work. Have pairs take turns asking and answering questions and filling in the chart with their partner's information.

5. Have students report on their partner's answers.

Practice 2

Class CD 2, Track 4

1. Have students read the directions for the activity and look at the phrases.

2. Play or read the example conversation twice.

   A: What do you usually do in the morning?
   B: I usually get up early in the morning.
   A: What about in the afternoon?
   B: I often play soccer in the afternoon.

3. Give students time to write what they do in the morning and afternoon on Saturday.

4. Pair Work. Have students take turns asking and answering questions about their answers.

Practice 3

1. Have students read the directions for the activity and look at the example.

2. Group Work. Have the class sit in groups of two pairs from Practice 2. Have one student from each pair tell the group one interesting thing about their partner.

3. Have one student from each group report on the group's answers.

Extension

Bring in magazine pictures of people doing various leisure-time activities. Draw a calendar of one month on the board. Mark a certain number of days to indicate one of the time adverbs and hold up one of the pictures. Have a volunteer make a sentence. Continue with other time adverbs and magazine pictures.

2. Talking about routines (2)

Review. Say one of the adverbs of time and an activity. Have a volunteer make a question and another volunteer answer. Continue with other activities and time adverbs.

Presentation

1. Have students look at the function box. Give them time to read the examples.

2. Model the exchanges and have students repeat chorally.

3. Practice a few exchanges with various students.

Notes

1. Explain that the question *Do you ever…?* is used to ask if something is done at any time for any amount of time.

2. Explain that *to have someone over* means to invite them to your home for a social occasion.

3. The function box includes many answer variations. Take some extra time to have students practice various exchanges so they practice each possible answer.

Practice 1

Class CD 2, Track 5

1. Have students read the directions for the activity and look at the pictures and phrases. Have students identify the activity in each picture.

2. Play or read the example conversation twice.

   A: Do you ever play sports on the weekend?
   B: Yes, I sometimes play tennis. Do you ever play sports on the weekend?
   A: No, not very often.

3. Pair Work. Have students take turns asking and answering questions about what they do on Saturday night.

4. Ask students to report on their partner's activities.

Practice 2

1. Have students read the directions for the activity and look at the example and the words in the box.

2. Give students time to write three other things they do. Brainstorm ideas, if necessary.

3. Pair Work. Have students take turns asking and answering questions about other things they do on Saturday night.

4. Have students report on their partner's answers.

Extension

Ask the class which classmate does the most interesting things on Saturday night. Ask students what they would like to do on Saturday night, but can't because of time or money constraints.

Listen to This

Class CD 2, Track 6

Part 1

1. Have students read the directions for the activity.

2. Play or read the conversation. Tell students to listen for how Angie feels about her job and check the answer.

   I: Wow. You're a model! That must be exciting!
   A: It's a lot of fun. I love it. But sometimes it's very tiring.
   I: Tiring? Why is that?
   A: Well I often have all-day shoots on Saturdays, and have to get up very early. I usually get up around 5:00 A.M., and then a car from the studio comes to pick me up at 6:00 and take me to the location.
   I: Does it take a long time to shoot the photos?
   A: Sometimes. The other models and I often have to change clothes ten or more times. And it takes about an hour to take all the photos with each set of clothes. So I often spend 10 or 12 hours on a photo shoot.
   I: I see.
   A: So I get home pretty late, and when I do, I'm really tired and hungry.
   I: I bet! And what about the clothes you model. Do you get to keep them?
   A: Unfortunately not! But the work pays really well. I sometimes make five or six hundred dollars for one day.
   I: That's pretty good. And do you work on Sundays, too?
   A: Not usually. But on Sundays I spend about four hours in the gym working out to keep in shape.
   I: So I guess you don't have time to see a movie next weekend?
   A: No, I'm sorry. But thanks for asking.

3. Ask volunteers for their answers.

   Answer:
   likes it a lot

Part 2

1. Have students read the directions for the activity and look at the chart. Go over any vocabulary students don't know.

2. Play or read the conversations again and tell students to listen for the details of Angie's schedule. Have students check if each statement in the chart is true or false.

3. Play or read the conversation again for students to check their answers.

4. Ask volunteers for their answers.

Answers:
1. true
2. true
3. false
4. true
5. false
6. false

Part 3

1. Have students read the directions for the activity.

2. Pair Work. Have pairs discuss if they would like to be a model and what they think the pros and cons are.

3. Ask volunteers for their answers.

Let's Talk

Part 1

1. Have students read the directions for the activity and look at the chart and the words in the box.

2. Give students time to write their information in the chart.

3. Circulate and help as needed.

Part 2

1. Have students read the directions for the activity and look at the example and the phrases in the box.

2. Class Work. Have students walk around the class asking each other about the information in their charts. Make sure they write the names of the people who do the same things they do.

3. Have students report on the information in their charts. Find out what were the most popular activities.

Extension

Have students use the library or Internet to research various high-profile jobs (model, movie star, company CEO, president, prime minister, etc.) and what kind of daily schedule they require. Students can do this individually or in groups. Have students report their findings to the class. Have the class discuss if they would like to have one of the jobs.

How was your weekend?

Vocabulary

Introduce these words and phrases to the students:

pretty good: very good

sunburned: red from being burned by the sun

Prelistening

1. Have students open their books and look at the photograph. Ask:

   - *What do the speakers have with them? Why?* (weekend bags; They are coming back from their weekends.)

2. Pair Work. Read the title of the conversation and the prelistening question. Have students take turns asking and answering the question.

3. Class Work. Have pairs share their answers with the class.

Conversation 2

Class CD 2, Track 7

1. With books closed, play the recording or read the conversation.

Jack:	How was your weekend, Mei-ho?
Mei-ho:	It was pretty good, thanks. How about you? Did you have a nice weekend?
Jack:	Yes, it was terrific.
Mei-ho:	What did you do?
Jack:	I went to the beach with my family. It was great.
Mei-ho:	How was the weather?
Jack:	Fantastic—sunny and hot.
Mei-ho:	So what did you do there?
Jack:	We walked along the beach and swam in the ocean. And then we had a barbecue on the beach on Saturday night. On Sunday I played tennis.
Mei-ho:	Oh … so that's why you're so sunburned!

2. Ask this comprehension question:

   - *In general, what are the speakers talking about?* (what they did over the weekend)

3. Say: *Listen again. This time listen to the details of the conversation.*

4. Play or read the conversation again, pausing for choral repetition. Allow students to write down the information as they listen. Play or read the conversation again, if needed, for students to get all the information.

5. Ask the following questions:

   - *How was Speaker 2's weekend?* (pretty good)
   - *How was Speaker 1's weekend?* (terrific)
   - *What did Speaker 1 do?* (went to the beach)
   - *How was the weather?* (sunny and hot)
   - *What did Speaker 1 do at the beach?* (walked along the beach, swam in the ocean, and had a barbecue)
   - *What did Speaker 1 do on Sunday?* (played tennis)
   - *What does Speaker 2 notice about Speaker 1?* (He is sunburned.)

   Elicit responses from various students.

PRONUNCIATION FOCUS

Class CD 2, Track 8

1. Explain what the focus is. Play or read the examples in the book and have students repeat chorally.

   How was your weekend?
   It was pretty good.
   How was the weather?
   It was terrific.

2. With books open, play or read the conversation again. Tell students to pay attention to the pronunciation of the word *was*.

3. Paired Reading. Have students practice the conversation, switching roles.

Give It a Try

1. Asking about the weekend

Presentation

1. Have students look at the function box. Give them time to read the examples.

2. Model the exchanges and have students repeat chorally.

3. Practice a few exchanges with various students.

Note

Tell students that another way to say *What did you do on the weekend?* is *What did you do over the weekend?* or *What did you do this weekend?* (if you are asking on Monday) or *What did you do last weekend?* (if you are asking on Tuesday through Friday).

Practice

Class CD 2, Track 9

1. Have students read the directions for the activity.

2. Play or read the example conversation twice.

   A: Hi, Paul. How was your weekend?
   B: It was OK thanks. How was yours?
   A: It was very quiet—nice and relaxing.
   B: That sounds good.

3. Group Work. Have students take turns greeting each other and asking about each other's weekend.

4. Have a student from each group report their discussion to the class.

2. Talking about past events (1)

Presentation

1. Have students look at the function box. Give them time to read the examples.

2. Model the exchanges and have students repeat chorally.

3. Practice a few exchanges with various students.

Practice

Class CD 2, Track 10

1. Have students read the directions for the activity and look at choices and the verbs in the box.

2. Play or read the example conversation twice.

   A: What did you do on the weekend?
   B: I visited friends. What did you do?
   A: I went to the beach.

3. Give students time to check what they did last weekend or write their own ideas.

4. Pair Work. Have students take turns asking and answering questions about what they did last weekend.

5. Have several pairs demonstrate their conversations for the class.

Extension

Have students write a funny or interesting story about what they did over the weekend. The story can be true or false. Have students tell their stories to the class and have the other students ask questions.

3. Talking about past events (2)

Presentation

1. Have students look at the function box. Give them time to read the examples.

2. Model the exchanges and have students repeat chorally.

3. Practice a few exchanges with various students.

Practice

Class CD 2, Track 11

1. Have students read the directions for the activity and look at the chart.

2. Give students time to check the things they did in the first column.

3. Play or read the example.

> A: Did you have a nice weekend?
> B: Yes, I did.
> A: Did you go the movies?
> B: No, I didn't. I went shopping. I bought some great CDs.

4. Pair Work. Have students take turns asking each other about the information in their chart. Have them write their partner's answers in the second column.

5. Have students report their partner's answers to the class.

Listen to This

Part 1

Class CD 2, Track 12

1. Have students read the directions for the activity and look at the choices.

2. Play or read the conversation twice. Tell students to check what Sami and Tamika are talking about. Make sure students understand that they should check what the general topic is, not everything they are talking about.

> S: How was your weekend Tamika?
> T: Pretty good, thanks.
> S: Did you go to the rock concert in the park?
> T: No, I didn't. Did you?
> S: No, I didn't either. But I heard it was terrific.
> T: Yeah, I heard it was fabulous. I saw a great movie though.
> S: Oh, me too. What did you see?
> T: I saw that new Tom Cruise movie. It's really good.
> S: Oh, good. I'm going to see it this weekend. I saw a Korean movie on Friday night. It was pretty good. Then after the movie I went to a club with some friends.

> T: Oh, yeah? And did you go to Janet's party on Saturday night?
> S: I wanted to, but I decided to study for my economics test.
> T: You are such a good student! I didn't go to the dance party either because it was my dad's birthday. We went out for a family dinner. Sunday was fun though because I played a great game of soccer.
> S: I didn't know you played soccer!
> T: Yeah, I do. It's fun. Did you get to play sports at all over the weekend?
> S: I wanted to, but I had a lot of things to do around the house.
> T: Too bad. I hate housework.
> S: Yeah, so do I.

3. Ask volunteers for the answers.

> **Answer:**
> weekends

Part 2

1. Have students read the directions for the activity and look at the chart.

2. Play or read the conversation again. Tell students to put an ✗ next to what Tamika and Sami did over the weekend. Tell them not to fill in the last row yet.

3. Play the conversation again for students to check their answers.

> **Answers:**
> Tamika: saw a movie; played soccer
> Sami: saw a movie; studied for a test

Part 3

1. Have students read the directions for the activity.

2. Play or read the conversation again and have students write what else Sami and Tamika did.

3. Ask volunteers for their answers.

> **Answers:**
> Sami: went to a club with friends; did housework
> Tamika: went out to dinner with family

Part 4

1. Have students read the directions for the activity.

2. Pair Work. Have students take turns comparing their weekends to Sami's and Tamika's.

Person to Person

Part 1

1. Have students read the instructions and look at the chart.

2. Give students time to fill in the first column of the chart. If students have trouble thinking of what to write in the chart, encourage them to use their imaginations to write something funny or interesting. You can also brainstorm ideas as a class.

3. Circulate and help as needed.

Part 2

1. Have students read the directions for the activity.

2. Pair Work. Have students take turns interviewing each other about what they wrote in their chart. Tell them to write their partner's information in the second column. When partners are finished interviewing each other, they should compare their answers.

Now Try This

1. Have students read the directions.

2. Give students time to think of the kinds of weekend activities that happen in their town or city.

3. Pair Work. Have students talk about the weekend activities that people often do in their town or city. Tell them to talk about what some of their favorite things to do are.

4. Class Work. Have the class compare their answers.

Extension

Have students look at the local newspaper to find out what is happening in their city or town this weekend. Have them plan a weekend for themselves and tell the class what they will do. They can also plan a weekend for a classmate.

Unit 8 Do you like coffee?

Components

Student Book, pages 62–69, 110
Class CD 2, Tracks 13–21
Optional Activities 8.1–8.2,
pages 110–111

Objectives

Functions: Asking about meals, asking about likes, asking about wants and preferences

Topics: Food and beverages, meals

Structures: Asking for something formally, *How about...? Do you like...? Wh-* questions

Pronunciation Focus: Intonation of questions

Listen to This: Listening to someone talk about food and ordering in a restaurant

---

Student Book page 62

CONSIDER THIS

1. Have students read the information and the question. Go over any vocabulary students don't know.

2. Group Work. Divide students into groups of four or five. Have students in each group take turns talking about which foods they would like to try. Help students with vocabulary as needed.

3. Ask volunteers to share their experiences with the class.

Prelistening

1. Pair Work. Have students open their books and look at the photograph. Have partners describe what they see to each other. Circulate and help with vocabulary as needed.

2. Class Work. Read the title of the conversation and the prelistening questions. Ask volunteers to answer the questions.

3. Pair Work. Have students take turns asking and answering the questions. Help with vocabulary as needed.

4. Class Work. Ask new volunteers to answer the questions. Find out if most of the class has big or small breakfasts by asking for a show of hands.

Conversation 1

Class CD 2, Track 13

1. With books closed, play the recording or read the conversation.

   Mike: What do you usually have for breakfast at home, Kenny?
   Kenny: I usually have rice and soup.
   Mike: Yeah? And what do you have to drink?
   Kenny: Oh, I usually have juice or milk.
   Mike: Do you like coffee?
   Kenny: Yes, it's OK. But I don't drink a lot of coffee.
   Mike: What's your favorite drink?
   Kenny: I guess it's soda.

2. Ask these comprehension questions:

   • *In general, what are the speakers talking about?* (what Speaker 2 usually has for breakfast)

3. Play or read the conversation again, pausing for choral repetition.

4. Ask the following questions:

   • *What does Speaker 2 usually have for breakfast?* (rice and soup)
   • *What does Speaker 2 drink?* (juice or milk)
   • *What does Speaker 2 think about coffee?* (It's OK.)
   • *What's Speaker 2's favorite drink?* (soda)

   Elicit responses from various students.

5. Paired Reading. Have students read the conversation, switching roles.

Give It a Try

1. Asking about meals

Presentation

1. Have students look at the function box. Give them time to read the examples.

2. Model the exchanges and have students repeat chorally.

3. Practice a few exchanges with various students.

Notes

1. Point out that *What do you have for breakfast?* means the same as *What do you eat for breakfast?*

2. Explain that fast food is very popular in the United States. Fast food is generally any food that is bought ready to eat in under ten minutes. It is also eaten very quickly. Discuss with students what is considered fast food in their country.

Practice 1

1. Have students read the directions for the activity and look at the chart.

2. Pair Work. Have pairs think of other items to add to the lists.

3. Have students report their items to the class. Write the new items on the board and conduct a class vote on which are the most popular foods and drinks.

Practice 2

Class CD 2, Track 14

1. Have students read the directions for the activity and look at the example conversation.

2. Play or read the example conversation twice.

   A: What do you have for breakfast?
   B: I usually have toast and fruit. What about you?
   A: I usually have rice and eggs. And what do you
      have to drink?
   B: I usually have coffee.

3. Pair Work. Have students take turns asking and answering questions about what they usually have for breakfast and lunch, and where they eat it.

2. Asking about likes

Review. Say a food or drink word. Have a student ask another student, *Do you usually have (toast) for breakfast?* The other student responds *Yes, I usually…/No, I don't usually…* Continue rapidly around the class.

Notes

Review stress in questions. On the board, write:

●
Do you like coffee?

Remind students that content words receive the most stress in a question. Have a volunteer come to the board and mark the content words in the question. Model the question and have students repeat. Have students repeat several times. Then have students practice the question substituting different food words.

Presentation

1. Have students look at the function box. Give them time to read the examples.

2. Model the exchanges and have students repeat chorally.

3. Practice a few exchanges with various students.

Practice 1

Class CD 2, Track 15

1. Have students read the directions for the activity and look at the pictures, labels, and the example.

2. Play or read the example twice.

   A: Do you like coffee?
   B: Not really. What about you?
   A: Yes, I do.

3. Pair Work. Have students take turns asking and answering questions about what foods they like.

4. Ask students to report on their partner's answers.

Practice 2

1. Have students read the directions for the activity and look at the chart and the words in the box. Help students with the vocabulary and pronunciation as needed.

2. Give students time to fill in the chart with information about their favorite foods.

3. Pair Work. Have students take turns asking and answering questions about their partner's favorite foods.

4. Have students report on their partner's answers.

Extension

Have students use their dictionaries to add more words to the Use These Words list.

Student Book page 65

Listen to This

Class CD 2, Track 16

Part 1

1. Have students read the directions for the activity.

2. Play or read the conversation. Tell students to listen for which meal they are talking about.

> R: Hi, Aran. Hey, I'm really hungry. I'm going to have a big breakfast today.
> A: Me too, Robert.
> R: What do people usually have for breakfast in Thailand, Aran?
> A: Well we don't really have a special meal for breakfast, like you do in many countries. We usually just have something that we cooked the night before for supper, you know, so there will always be rice of course, and usually some vegetable dish, and then maybe a curry dish, like curried chicken or beef. And tea or coffee to drink.
> R: Mmm. Sounds delicious.
> A: Yeah, but I usually just have a western breakfast— you know toast, coffee, and some fruit. How about in the UK?
> R: Well a typical English breakfast—that's difficult—it depends on what part of the country you live in, but I guess I can say people will have fried eggs, sausages, bacon, fried mushrooms, and tomatoes—everything fried so it's rather heavy. And tea with toast.
> A: So is that what you have?
> R: No. I have two boiled eggs, cereal, and juice.
> A: Very healthy!

3. Ask volunteers for their answer.

> **Answer:**
> breakfast

Part 2

1. Have students read the directions for the activity and look at the chart. Go over any vocabulary students don't know.

2. Play or read the conversation again and tell students to listen for the specific foods that people eat for breakfast in England and in Thailand. Have students put a ✓ next to the foods people eat in these countries.

3. Play or read the conversation again for students to check their answers.

4. Ask volunteers for their answers.

> **Answers:**
> Thailand: beef curry; chicken curry; coffee; rice; tea; vegetables
> England: bacon; fried eggs; fried mushrooms; sausages; tomatoes; toast; tea

Part 3

1. Have students read the directions for the activity.

2. Play or read the conversation and tell students to listen for what Aran and Robert eat for breakfast. Have students put an ✗ next to the foods they eat.

3. Play or read the conversation again for students to check their answers.

4. Ask volunteers for their answers.

> **Answers:**
> Aran: toast; coffee; fruit
> Robert: boiled eggs; cereal; juice

Part 4

1. Have students read the directions.

2. Play or read the conversation again, if necessary.

3. Pair work. Have students talk about what foods they eat for breakfast.

4. Have students report on their discussions to the class.

Let's Talk

Part 1

1. Have students read the directions for the activity and look at the chart.

2. Give students time to write their own idea, and their own information in the chart in the first column.

3. Circulate and help as needed.

Part 2

1. Have students read the directions for the activity and look at the example.

2. Group Work. Have students ask their classmates about their favorite foods and write the person's name and their response in the second column of the chart.

Part 3

1. Have students read the directions for the activity.

2. Have students look over their charts to see which foods most people in their group liked. Ask volunteers to report on the similarities they noticed in their group.

Extension

Ask students what other country's food they enjoy. Ask which countries they have traveled to and if they liked the food there.

Are you hungry?

Student Book page 66

Vocabulary

Introduce these words and phrase to the students:

What do you feel like?: What do you want to eat?

That sounds good: That's a good idea.

Prelistening

1. Have students open their books and look at the photograph. Ask:

   • *Where are the speakers?* (on a sidewalk outside a building)

2. Pair Work. Read the title of the conversation and the prelistening questions. Have students take turns asking and answering the questions.

4. Class Work. Ask new volunteers to answer the questions. Make a list on the board of students' answers.

Conversation 2

Class CD 2, Track 17

1. With books closed, play the recording or read the conversation.

   Jodi: Are you hungry?
   Kenny: Yes, I am.
   Jodi: Me too. Let's have something to eat.
   Kenny: What do you feel like?
   Jodi: How about some cake and a cappuccino?
   Kenny: OK.
   Jodi: Let's go to the Starlight Cafe. They have delicious cakes and great cappuccino.
   Kenny: That sounds good. Let's go.

2. Ask this comprehension question:

   • *In general, what are the speakers talking about?* (getting something to eat)

3. Say: *Listen again. This time listen to the details of the conversation.*

4. Play or read the conversation again, pausing for choral repetition. Allow students to write down the information as they listen. Play or read the conversation again, if needed, for students to get all the information.

5. Ask the following questions:

   • *How does Speaker 1 feel?* (hungry)
   • *What does Speaker 1 want to have?* (cake and cappuccino)
   • *Where do they want to go? Why?* (the Starlight Cafe; The cake and cappuccino are good there.)

Elicit responses from various students.

PRONUNCIATION FOCUS

Class CD 2, Track 18

1. Explain what the focus is. Play or read the examples in the book and have students repeat chorally.

   Are you hungry?
   What do you feel like?
   How about some cake and a cappuccino?

2. With books open, play or read the conversation again. Tell students to pay attention to the intonation of the questions.

3. Paired Reading. Have students practice the conversation, switching roles.

Give It a Try

1. Asking about wants and preferences

Presentation

1. Have students look at the function box. Give them time to read the examples.

2. Model the exchanges and have students repeat chorally.

3. Practice a few exchanges with various students.

Notes

1. Point out to students that *Would you like…?* is a more formal way of asking *Do you want…?*

2. Practice the difference in intonation in *Would you…?* questions and *What would…?* questions. On the board, write:

   Would you like something to eat?

   What would you like to eat?

   Mark the intonation. As you model the questions, emphasize the rising intonation at the end of the first question and falling intonation at the end of the second. Have students practice with several examples.

3. Point out to students that putting *please* at the end of a request makes it more polite. *(I'd like a burger, please.)*

Practice 1

Class CD 2, Track 19

1. Have students read the directions for the activity and look at the pictures, labels, and the words in the box.

2. Play or read the example conversation twice.

   A: Are you hungry?
   B: Yes, I am
   A: What do you feel like?
   B: Maybe a milk shake.

3. Pair Work. Have students take turns asking and answering whether they are hungry or thirsty and about what they feel like eating or drinking. They should practice using both the words in the box (for what they feel like generally—something hot/cold/light/sweet), and also the specific items pictured. *(I feel like something cold—maybe some iced tea.)*

4. Have several pairs demonstrate their conversation for the class.

Practice 2

Class CD 2, Track 20

1. Have students read the directions for the activity and look at the example conversation.

2. Play or read the example conversation twice.

   A: Would you like something to eat?
   B: No, not right now.
   A: Would you like something to drink?
   B: Yes, please. I'd like a milk shake.

3. Pair Work. Have students take turns asking and answering questions about the food in Practice 1. Make sure they are asking and answering more formally.

4. Have several pairs demonstrate their conversation for the class.

Extension

Class Discussion. Have the class discuss what their favorite snacks are. Explain that *comfort food* is food you eat when you want to feel good. Comfort food tends to have a lot of sugar, salt, and/or fat. Ask students what their favorite comfort foods are.

Practice 3

1. Have students read the directions for the activity and look at the chart.

2. Group Work. Have students take turns taking lunch orders from the others in their group.

3. Class Work. Have students go to students in another group and compare lists.

4. Have students report their lists to the class. Keep a tally on the board of what is ordered to find out what the most popular lunches are.

Listen to This

Class CD 2, Track 21

Part 1

1. Have students read the directions for the activity and look at the choices.

2. Play or read the conversation. Tell students to listen for what meal the speakers are eating.

   S: Are you ready to order?
   M: Yes, I'd like a chicken salad, please.
   S: Sure. And would you like bread with that?
   M: OK.
   S: What kind of dressing would you like?
   M: I'll have Italian. And for dessert I'd like a slice of chocolate cake.
   S: Fine. Would you like anything to drink?
   M: Yes. I'd like iced coffee, please.
   S: With cream?
   M: No, black please and plenty of ice.
   S: Certainly. And how about you, sir?
   P: I'll have the club sandwich, please.
   S: And would you like french fries with that?
   P: Yes, please.
   S: Anything else?
   P: I'd like juice. What kind of juices do you have?
   S: We have orange, tomato, apple, and grapefruit.
   P: I'd like apple juice please, but with no ice, please.
   S: OK. Thank you.

3. Ask volunteers for the answers.

   Answer:
   lunch or dinner

Part 2

1. Have students read the directions for the activity and look at the menu. Go over any items they don't know.

2. Play or read the conversation again. Tell students to write an *M* next to what Maria orders and *P* next to what Paul orders.

3. Play the conversation again for students to check their answers.

   Answers:
   Maria: chicken salad; bread; Italian dressing; chocolate cake; iced coffee
   Paul: club sandwich; french fries; apple juice

Part 3

1. Have students read the directions for the activity.

2. Group Work. Divide the class into groups of three. Have each group decide who will be the server and the two customers. Have them role-play the conversation. Tell them it doesn't have to be exactly like the recording, but it should be similar. Play or read the conversation again, if necessary.

3. Have several groups demonstrate the conversation for the class.

Extension

Make a different menu or have students make their own menus. Divide the class into groups of three and have them do their own role plays of ordering in a restaurant. Have several groups demonstrate for the class.

Person to Person

Part 1

1. Divide the class into pairs and have students decide who will be Student A (the customer) and who will be Student B (the server). Have Student B look at page 110.

2. Have students read the directions and look at the menus.

3. To check comprehension, ask:

   Student A, What is one question you will ask your partner about the menu? (What kind of eggs do you have?) Give Student A time to think about or write the questions they will ask Student B.

   Student B, How will you answer Student A's question? (We have fried, poached, boiled, and scrambled eggs.)

4. Pair Work. Have Student A ask Student B questions about the menu, and have Student B respond.

Part 2

1. Have students read the directions.

2. Pair Work. Have Student A order something and Student B take notes.

3. Have Student B tell the class what Student A wants to eat as if they were telling the cook in the kitchen.

Part 3

1. Have students read the directions for the activity.

2. Pair Work. Have partners reverse roles and role-play ordering breakfast and taking the order.

3. Have Student A tell the class what Student B wants to eat as if they were telling the cook in the kitchen.

Now Try This

1. Have students read the directions.

2. Give students time to make a simple breakfast menu.

3. Pair Work. Have students take turns ordering breakfast from their partner's menu.

Extension

Have pairs switch their menus with another pair. Have students talk about the differences and similarities in the menus. Ask students to choose which restaurant they think is better and why.

Components

Student Book, pages 70–77, 111
Class CD 2, Tracks 22–31
Optional Activities 9.1–9.2,
page 111

Objectives

Functions: Describing qualities,
asking about abilities and talents,
describing abilities

Topics: Hobbies, personal qualities

Structures: Adjectives, *Are you…?*
Can you…? What…?

Pronunciation Focus: Pronunciation
of *can* and *can't*

Listen to This: Listening to someone
talk about talents and hobbies

Student Book page 70

CONSIDER THIS

1. Have students read the information and the questions. Go over any vocabulary students don't know.

2. Group Work. Divide students into groups of four or five. Have students in each group take turns asking and answering the questions. Help students with vocabulary as needed.

3. Have students talk about which studies and hobbies they would like to try.

Vocabulary

Introduce these words and phrases to the students:

Congratulations: what you say to someone when they have completed something successfully or on a special day such as a birthday or anniversary

patient: having a calm and unrushed attitude

subject: the person or object that you are taking a picture of

creative: using your imagination

original: one of a kind; unique

Prelistening

1. Pair Work. Have students open their books and look at the photograph. Have partners describe what they see to each other. Circulate and help with vocabulary as needed.

2. Class Work. Read the title of the conversation and the prelistening questions. Ask volunteers to answer the questions.

3. Pair Work. Have students take turns asking and answering the questions. Help with vocabulary as needed.

4. Class Work. Ask new volunteers to answer the questions. Make a list on the board of students' hobbies.

Conversation 1

Class CD 2, Track 22

1. With books closed, play the recording or read the conversation.

   Aya: Congratulations, Julia. You are a really good photographer.
   Julia: Thanks.
   Aya: So how do you take a good photograph?
   Julia: Well, you need to be patient. It takes time to get a good picture. You need good light and a good subject.
   Aya: And I guess you need to be creative. Your photos are always very original.
   Julia: Well, I try to be different.
   Aya: I never seem to take good photos. I don't think I'm very artistic. And I'm not very patient.
   Julia: Well, it's easy to learn. Do you want me to give you some lessons?
   Aya: Yeah. That would be great.

2. Ask this comprehension question:

   • *Why does Speaker 1 congratulate Speaker 2?* (Speaker 2's photo won an award.)

3. Play or read the conversation again, pausing for choral repetition.

4. Ask the following questions:
   - *What quality does Speaker 2 say you need to be a good photographer?* (patience)
   - *What else do you need to take a good picture?* (good light and a good subject)
   - *How does Speaker 1 describe Speaker 2's photos?* (original)
   - *How does Speaker 1 describe herself?* (not artistic and not patient)
   - *What does Speaker 2 offer to do?* (to give Speaker 1 photography lessons)

   Elicit responses from various students.

5. Paired Reading. Have students read the conversation, switching roles.

Student Book page 71

Give It a Try

1. Describing qualities

Presentation

1. Have students look at the function box. Give them time to read the examples.

2. Model the examples and have students repeat chorally.

3. Practice a few examples with various students.

Notes
Review stress of content words in a sentence. On the board, write:

$$\overset{\bullet}{A\ photographer}\ needs\ to\ be\ \overset{\bullet}{patient.}$$

$$\overset{\bullet}{A\ teacher}\ needs\ to\ be\ \overset{\bullet}{flexible}\ and\ \overset{\bullet}{tolerant.}$$

$$\overset{\bullet}{A\ doctor}\ needs\ to\ be\ \overset{\bullet}{smart,}\ \overset{\bullet}{serious,}\ and\ \overset{\bullet}{well\text{-}organized.}$$

Remind students that the content words are the words that give the important information in a sentence. Have volunteers come to the board and mark the content words in each sentence. Model each sentence and have students repeat.

Practice 1

Class CD 2, Track 23

1. Have students read the directions for the activity and look at the pictures, the examples, and the list of adjectives.

2. Review the meanings of the adjectives. Have students either use each in a sentence or say a synonym.

3. Play or read the example twice.

   A: A photographer needs to be patient.
   B: He also needs to be artistic.

4. Give students time to think of three adjectives for each occupation and rank them. You may suggest they use another piece of paper to write their answers. For example:

   Teacher: 1. smart   2. well-organized   3. tolerant

5. Pair Work. Have students compare their answers.

6. Have students report their partner's answers to the class.

Practice 2

Class CD 2, Track 24

1. Have students read the directions for the activity and look at the chart and the words in the box. Go over any words students don't know. Brainstorm other adjectives, if necessary.

2. Play or read the example twice.

   A: I'm patient and easygoing. But sometimes I'm forgetful.

3. Give students time to write their positive and negative qualities in the chart. Encourage them to use adjectives from Practice 1, as well as from the word box and other words they know.

4. Pair Work. Have students discuss their answers with a partner.

5. Have students present their partner's answers to the class.

Extension

As a class, write synonyms and antonyms for each adjective. Divide the class into teams. Say a word and "synonym" or "antonym" and have one person from each team try to be the first to say the synonym or antonym. Play to a point or time limit.

2. Asking about abilities and talents

Review. Say an adjective. Point to a student and have them use the word in a sentence that shows they know what the word means. Move rapidly around the class.

Presentation

1. Have students look at the function box. Give them time to read the examples.

2. Model the exchanges and have students repeat chorally.

3. Practice a few exchanges with various students.

Notes

1. Review intonation of *Are you…?* questions. On the board, write:

Are you creative?

Are you good at languages?

Remind students that the intonation in these questions rises at the end. Mark the intonation in the questions. Model and have students repeat.

2. Explain that *somewhat* means not a small amount, but not a big amount either.

Practice 1

1. Have students read the directions for the activity and look at the chart.

2. Give students time to check their skills in the chart.

Practice 2

Class CD 2, Track 25

1. Have students read the directions for the activity.

2. Play or read the example conversation twice.

   A: Are you creative?
   B: No, I'm not very creative. Are you good at languages?
   A: Yes, I'm pretty good at languages.

3. Pair Work. Have students ask at least two questions to each other. Brainstorm possible questions first, if necessary. (*Have you always been good at math? Do you have/Do you want a job that uses your math ability?*)

Practice 3

1. Have students read the directions for the activity.

2. Group Work. Have students tell the class about at least one person in their group.

Extension

Have the class discuss their own special qualities and which occupation would be the best for them. Have the other students try to think of other occupations that would also be a good match.

Listen to This

Class CD 2, Track 26

Part 1

1. Have students read the directions for the activity and look at the choices.

2. Play or read the conversation. Tell students to listen for which people Carl is talking about.

   A: So tell me about your family, Carl.
   C: Well, I have one sister and one brother.
   A: And what do they do?
   C: My sister Rosa teaches ballroom dancing.
   A: Really? Does she have her own dance school?
   C: No, but she teaches for the biggest school in our town.
   A: She must be a very good dancer.
   C: Yes, she is. She's also a good singer. She sings in a band when she has free time. And she also has a part-time job teaching German and Russian.
   A: That's amazing. She sounds very talented—and busy!
   C: Yes, she is always running around doing things. She never stops
   A: Really? And how about your brother?
   C: He's a junior at the State University. He's very smart. He's studying engineering.
   A: Has he always been a good student?
   C: Yeah. He's very good at math and computer science. He loves studying. He's never been interested in sports. Once he starts reading a book, he won't put it down. Sometimes it drives my parents crazy, because when he's studying or reading, he forgets everything else. Sometimes he doesn't even remember to eat lunch!

3. Ask volunteers for their answer.

   Answer:
   sister and brother

Part 2

1. Have students read the directions for the activity and look at the chart.

2. Play or read the conversation again and tell students to listen for the specific talents of each person. Have students put a ✓ in the correct columns.

3. Play or read the conversation again for students to check their answers.

4. Ask volunteers for their answers.

   Answers:
   Rosa: Languages; Music; Dancing
   Peter: Math; Computers

Part 3

1. Have students read the directions for the activity.

2. Pair Work. Have students discuss if they are more similar to Rosa or to Peter. Play or read the conversation again, if necessary.

3. Have students report on their discussion to the class.

Let's Talk

Part 1

1. Have students read the directions for the activity and look at the chart.

2. Give students time to write information about their mother, father, and best friend in the chart.

3. Circulate and help as needed.

Part 2

1. Have students read the directions for the activity.

2. Pair Work. Have students take turns asking each other about the information in their charts.

3. Have students tell the class about their partner's mother, father, and best friend.

Extension

Divide the class into small groups. Have groups discuss which qualities or talents they wish they had.

Can you play the guitar?

Vocabulary

Introduce these words and phrases to the students:

pretty hard: difficult

not that hard: not too difficult

Prelistening

1. Have students open their books and look at the photograph. Ask:

   • *What are the speakers doing?* (talking about music/having a music lesson)

2. Pair Work. Read the title of the conversation and the prelistening questions. Have students take turns asking and answering the questions.

3. Class Work. Ask new volunteers to answer the questions. Make a list on the board of musical instruments that students play.

Conversation 2

Class CD 2, Track 27

1. With books closed, play the recording or read the conversation.

   Tim: Wow! You can play the guitar really well.
   Aya: Thanks. Can you play the guitar?
   Tim: No, I can't. But I can play the violin.
   Aya: Really? What else can you play?
   Tim: I can play the trumpet, too.
   Aya: Oh, yeah? I can't play the trumpet. I think it's pretty hard.
   Tim: It's not that hard. You just need to practice.
   Aya: Can I hear you play some time?
   Tim: Sure.

2. Ask this comprehension question:

   • *In general, what are the speakers talking about?* (playing musical instruments)

3. Say: *Listen again. This time listen to the details of the conversation.*

4. Play or read the conversation again, pausing for choral repetition. Allow students to write down the information as they listen. Play or read the conversation again, if needed, for students to get all the information.

5. Ask the following questions:

   • *What instrument does Speaker 2 play?* (guitar)
   • *Does Speaker 2 play the guitar well?* (yes)
   • *Can Speaker 1 play the guitar?* (no)
   • *What instruments does Speaker 1 play?* (violin and trumpet)
   • *Does Speaker 2 play the trumpet? Why not?* (no; It's pretty hard.)
   • *What does Speaker 2 ask Speaker 1?* (if she can hear him play)

   Elicit responses from various students.

PRONUNCIATION FOCUS

Class CD 2, Track 28

1. Explain what the focus is. Play or read the examples in the book and have students repeat chorally.

   Can you play the guitar?
   I can play the violin.
   I can't play the trumpet.

2. With books open, play or read the conversation again. Tell students to pay attention to the pronunciation of the words *can* and *can't*.

3. Paired Reading. Have students practice the conversation, switching roles.

Give It a Try

1. Describing abilities (1)

Presentation

1. Have students look at the function box. Give them time to read the examples.

2. Model the exchanges and have students repeat chorally.

3. Practice a few exchanges with various students.

Notes

1. Make sure students understand the difference in usage between *good* and *well*. Explain that *good* is an adjective that describes a noun and *well* is an adverb that describes a verb. On the board, write:

   She is a good singer.

   She sings well.

   Ask volunteers to come to the board and underline the adjective and adverb and circle the noun and the verb. This is an important grammar rule, so have students write a few of their own sentence pairs and read them to the class.

2. Review intonation of *Can you…?* questions. On the board, write:

   Can you play the guitar?

   Can he play the piano?

   Remind students that the intonation in these questions rises at the end. Mark the intonation in the questions. Model and have students repeat.

3. Practice combining sentences. On the board, write:

   I can play the piano. I can't play the violin.

   I can play the piano. I can play the trumpet.

   Have student volunteers come to the board and combine the two sentence pairs into one sentence:

   I can play the piano, but I can't play the violin.

   I can play the piano and the trumpet.

   Make sure students understand that in the second pair, *I can play* does not have to be repeated in the second half of the sentence. Have students practice combining their own sentences.

Practice 1

Class CD 2, Track 29

1. Have students read the directions for the activity and look at the chart and the example.

2. Play or read the example conversation twice.

   A: Can you play hockey?
   B: No, I can't. Can you?
   A: Not very well.

3. Give students time to check their answers in the chart.

4. Group Work. Have students take turns asking each other about the information in their charts.

Practice 2

1. Have students read the directions for the activity.

2. Have students tell the class at least two things people in their group can do and about two things they can't do.

2. Describing abilities (2)

Presentation

1. Have students look at the function box. Give them time to read the example questions.

2. Model the questions and have students repeat chorally.

3. Practice by having various students answer the questions you ask with their own information.

Note

Review intonation of *What…?* questions. On the board, write:

What instrument can you play?

What languages can you speak?

Remind students that the intonation in these questions goes down at the end. Mark the intonation in the questions. Model and have students repeat.

Practice 1

Class CD 2, Track 30

1. Have students read the directions for the activity and look at the chart.

2. Play or read the example conversation twice.

   A: What musical instrument can you play?
   B: I can play the piano. What languages can you speak?
   A: I can speak Chinese and English.

3. Group Work. Divide the class into groups of four. Have students take turns asking each other the questions in the chart. Have students fill in the chart with their classmates' names and abilities.

Practice 2

1. Have students read the directions for the activity and look at the example.

2. Have students take turns telling the class three facts about the people from their group.

Listen to This

Class CD 2, Track 31

Part 1

1. Have students read the directions for the activity and look at the choices.

2. Play or read the conversation. Tell students to listen for where Sonia and Mike are.

   M: Wow, Sonia. You're borrowing a lot of books for the weekend.
   S: Well, I love reading. And there are some great books in this library.
   M: Yes, there are. I see you have some books in Spanish. Your Spanish must be pretty good.
   S: It is, I guess. I can speak and read it fluently.
   M: Wow. And do you know any other languages?
   S: Well, French, but my French isn't very good. How about you?
   M: I speak a little German and I'm studying Korean this year.
   S: Interesting.
   M: Yeah, but I'm just a beginner in both languages.
   S: And I see you're borrowing some music CDs.
   M: Yeah. I play guitar, and I want to listen to some good guitar music. I teach guitar as well.
   S: Really? Are you good at any other instruments?
   M: Not really. Just guitar. How about you?
   S: I play piano pretty well and I'm learning violin this year. It's fun but I'm finding it really difficult.
   M: What other plans do you have for the weekend?
   S: Well, I'm going to play some tennis. I'm playing in a tournament on Sunday.
   M: Is that right? Is your tennis good?
   S: I guess so. Do you play tennis?
   M: I do, but not very well. My best sport is baseball. Do you play any other sports?
   S: Not really.

3. Ask volunteers for the answers.

Answer:
library

Part 2

1. Have students read the directions for the activity and look at the chart.

2. Play or read the conversation again. Tell students to circle the correct answers for each person.

3. Play the conversation again for students to check their answers.

> **Answers:**
> Sonia: Spanish; French/piano; violin/tennis
> Mike: German; Korean/guitar/tennis; baseball

Part 3

1. Have students read the directions for the activity.

2. Have students write a + next to the things the people can do well and a – for things they can't do as well. Play the conversation again if necessary.

3. Pair Work. Have students compare their abilities to Sonia and Mike.

4. Have students report on their discussion to the class.

Extension

Have students write a very short imaginary biography about themselves. The biography should make them sound very famous, interesting, and talented. Tell them that it should describe their personalities, what talents they have, and things that they have done. Have students read their biographies to the class.

Student Book pages 77 & 111

Person to Person

Part 1

1. Divide the class into pairs and have students decide who will be Student A and who will be Student B. Have Student B look at page 111.

2. Have students read the directions and look at the two job ads.

3. Give Students A time to choose the special skills or abilities a person needs for each job. Give Students B time to look at the two job ads and decide which one they think they are most qualified for.

4. Circulate and help as needed.

Part 2

1. Have students read the directions.

2. Pair Work. Have Student A ask Student B about his or her skills. Student A listens to Student B's responses, then tells him or her which job is best for him or her.

3. Have several pairs role-play for the class.

Part 3

1. Have students read the directions and look at the two job ads.

2. Give Students B time to choose the special skills or abilities a person needs for each job. Give Students A time to look at the two job ads and decide which one they are most qualified for.

3. Circulate and help as needed.

Part 4

1. Have students read the directions.

2. Have Student B ask Student A about his or her skills. Student B listens to Student A's responses then tells him or her which job is best for him or her.

3. Have several pairs role-play for the class.

Now Try This

1. Have students read the questions.

2. Have a class discussion about the special hobbies and activities of the students' countries and the skills they require.

Extension

Write different occupations on separate slips of paper. Divide the class into groups of three. Have one student from each group choose a paper. Have the group role-play one of them applying for that job and the other two interviewing him/her.

Review:
Units 7–9

Components

Student Book, pages 78–79
Class CD 2, tracks 32–34

Listen to This Unit 7

Class CD 2, Track 32

Part 1

1. Have students read the directions and look at the chart.

2. Play or read the conversation. Have students check how Ken liked the things in the chart.

   A: So how was your vacation, Ken?
   K: Oh, pretty good thanks. But I bought a lot of postcards. Would you like to see them?
   A: Hmm. Maybe next time. How was the hotel?
   K: It was fantastic. Very comfortable and very good service.
   A: That's good. And was the weather good?
   K: Not all of the time. It rained a few days, so it was a bit disappointing. But there were some nice days as well.
   A: And did you have a good flight back?
   K: Oh, it was horrible! The plane was full and the food was terrible.

3. Play or read the conversation again for students to check their answers.

   Answers:
   1. The hotel: Good
   2. The weather: So-so
   3. The flight: Not good

Part 2

1. Pair Work. Have students compare their answers.

2. Ask several students for their answers.

Give It a Try

1. Have students read the directions. Give them time to think of follow-up questions.

2. Pair Work. Have students take turns asking the questions and answering them.

3. Have several pairs demonstrate for the class.

Listen to This Unit 8

Class CD 2, Track 33

Part 1

1. Have students read the directions and look at the chart.

2. Play or read the conversation. Have students put a ✓ next to the food each place serves and how good it is.

   J: So what do you feel like eating?
   S: I'm not sure. Any suggestions?
   J: What do you feel like? Are you hungry?
   S: Yes, I'm pretty hungry.
   J: Well, Jenny's Kitchen has sandwiches and hot dogs.
   S: What's their food like?
   J: It's pretty cheap. I guess it's average. It's not the best place around here actually.
   S: Hmm. Any place better you know?
   J: Well, would you like to have noodles? Bob's Cafe has noodles and they also serve sushi. I was there last week and their food is terrific.
   S: Umm, I don't really feel like noodles or sushi.
   J: Boy, you are hard to please. Oh, I know another place. Do you know The Snack Shack?
   S: No. What do they have there?
   J: They have great pizza!
   S: Pizza sounds good to me.
   J: OK. Let's go there.

3. Play or read the conversation again for students to check their answers.

4. Ask several students for the answers.

   Answers:
Jenny's Kitchen:	Sandwiches; Hot dogs/So-so
Bob's Cafe:	Noodles; Sushi/Great
The Snack Shack:	Pizza/Great

Part 2

1. Have students read the directions.

2. Pair Work. Have students tell each other where Jay and Sally decided to eat and see if they came up with the same answer.

   Answer:
   The Snack Shack

Give It a Try

1. Have students read the directions.

2. Group Work. Have students discuss their favorite foods and drinks and write them down.

3. Ask a student from each group to report their group's discussion to the class.

Listen to This Unit 9

Class CD 2, Track 34

Part 1

1. Have students read the directions and look at the chart. Review the adjectives, if necessary.

2. Play or read the conversation.

C: Well, I've met two possible roommates, and now I have to decide who I like better.

T: Well, Cassy, let's start with you first. What are you like? That will help you to figure out who you'll get along with better.

C: Well, I think I'm easy to get along with. Don't you?

T: Well, yes, you're easygoing. You're also very reliable—always there when somebody needs you. And you're very neat and well-organized.

C: That's true. I don't like being with people who are sloppy or lazy.

T: OK. So who was the first person you met?

C: Her name is Kavita. She's very neat. Her room in the dormitory is always clean and organized.

T: Right. She's very energetic too, isn't she? She always seems to be working. She never takes any time off. Do you think she's too serious?

C: Well, maybe. But at least I know she's not lazy. And she's very reliable. That's important to me.

T: Now who was the other person? Soon-Ya?

C: That's right. He's very funny. I love his sense of humor.

T: Yeah. He's really creative, too. He's a talented musician, and a good artist as well.

C: You're right. But I don't think he's very neat. His room is always a mess. And he's not so reliable at times. He often forgets appointments.

T: So who do you think your new roommate is going to be?

3. Have students check the qualities that each person has.

4. Play or read the conversation again for students to check their answers.

Answers:
Cassy: well-organized; easygoing; reliable
Kavita: well-organized; serious; energetic; reliable
Soon-Ya: sloppy; funny; creative

Part 2

1. Pair Work. Have students discuss the question.

2. Ask several students for their answers and why they think Cassy should choose the person they did.

Give It a Try

1. Have students read the directions and look at the questions.

2. Pair Work. Have students take turns asking each other the questions and then recommending a job.

3. Have students tell the class what job they recommended and why. Have the partner say if they agree or not and why.

Let's have coffee.

Components

Student Book, pages 80–87, 112
Class CD 2, Tracks 35–43
Optional Activities 10.1–10.2,
pages 111–112

Objectives

Functions: Asking about places, describing outdoor locations, giving directions

Topics: Places in a town, directions

Structures: Prepositions of location, adverbs of movement, *Is there…?* *Where…?*

Pronunciation Focus: Stress in compound nouns

Listen to This: Listening to someone talk about places and directions

---

Student Book page 80

CONSIDER THIS

1. Have students read the information and the questions. Go over any vocabulary students don't know.

2. Group Work. Divide students into groups of four or five. Have students in each group take turns asking and answering the questions. Help students with vocabulary as needed.

3. Have students talk about their coffee habits and other drink preferences.

Vocabulary

Introduce these words and phrases to the students:

just around the corner: very close by on the next street

Whereabouts?: Where?

Do you feel like…?: Do you want to…?

have a look: go and see something, usually for the first time

Sounds good: a way to express agreement with plans

Prelistening

1. Pair Work. Have students open their books and look at the photograph. Have partners describe what they see to each other. Circulate and help with vocabulary as needed.

2. Class Work. Read the title of the conversation and the prelistening questions. Ask volunteers to answer the questions.

3. Pair Work. Have students take turns asking and answering the questions. Help with vocabulary as needed.

4. Class Work. Ask new volunteers to answer the questions. Find out what most of the class likes to drink by making a list on the board.

Conversation 1

Class CD 2, Track 35

1. With books closed, play the recording or read the conversation.

   Arun: I'd love some coffee. Is there a coffee shop around here?

   Beth: Yeah, there's one just around the corner.

   Arun: Really. Whereabouts?

   Beth: It's next to the bookstore. It's called Dove.

   Arun: Oh, yeah. Do you feel like having a cup of coffee?

   Beth: Sure. And after that I'd like to have a look at that new music store.

   Arun: Where's that?

   Beth: It's on Forbes Street, near the subway entrance.

   Arun: OK. Sounds good.

2. Ask this comprehension question:

   • *What are the speakers going to do?* (go for a cup of coffee)

3. Play or read the conversation again, pausing for choral repetition.

4. Ask the following questions:

- *Is the coffee shop near? How do you know?* (yes; Speaker 2 says it's just around the corner.)
- *Where is it exactly?* (next to the bookstore)
- *What's the name of the coffee shop?* (Dove)
- *What does Speaker 2 want to do after having coffee?* (go to the new music store)
- *Where is the music store?* (on Forbes Street, near the subway entrance)

Elicit responses from various students.

5. Paired Reading. Have students read the conversation, switching roles.

Student Book page 81

Give It a Try

1. Asking about places

Presentation

1. Have students look at the function box. Give them time to read the examples.

2. Model the exchanges and have students repeat chorally.

3. Practice a few exchanges with various students.

Notes

1. Explain that *around here* means the same as *near here*.

2. Review intonation of *Is there…?* questions. On the board, write:

Is there a coffee shop around here?

Is there a music store around here?

Remind students that the intonation in these questions rises at the end. Mark the intonation in the questions. Model and have students repeat.

Practice 1

Class CD 2, Track 36

1. Have students read the directions for the activity and look at the map and the list of places.

2. Play or read the example conversation twice.

A: Is there a supermarket around here?
B: Yes, there is. It's on the corner of Oak Avenue and Seventh Street.

3. Pair Work. Have students take turns asking about the places on the list and telling where each is on the map.

4. Have pairs demonstrate their conversation for the class.

Practice 2

1. Have students read the directions for the activity and look at the example conversation and the words in the box.

2. Pair Work. Have students take turns asking each other about places in their neighborhoods.

3. Have students tell the class about a place in their partner's neighborhood. (*John has a coffee shop just around the corner from him, on Mansilla Street.*)

Extension

Divide the class into groups of three or four. Have one student quickly sketch a map of an imaginary neighborhood, but not show the rest of the group. Have the student describe the neighborhood while the other students in the group draw a map of it. When they are finished, have the group compare their maps for accuracy. Continue until each student in the group has described a neighborhood.

2. Describing outdoor locations

Review. Draw a map of a neighborhood on the board. Point to a student and have them say one sentence about the neighborhood. Continue rapidly with other students.

Presentation

1. Have students look at the function box. Give them time to read the examples.

2. Model the questions and have students repeat chorally.

3. Have students look at each illustration of the prepositions of location and repeat them chorally.

4. Practice a few exchanges with various students.

5. Have students close their books. Dictate one of the prepositional phrases and have students draw a simple picture that illustrates it. Circulate and check answers.

Practice 1

Class CD 2, Track 37

1. Have students read the directions for the activity and look at the map and list of places.

2. Play or read the example conversation twice.

   A: Where's the coffee shop?
   B: It's on the corner of Pine Street and 5th Avenue.

3. Pair Work. Have students take turns asking and answering questions about the location of the places on the list.

4. Ask volunteers to repeat their conversations for the class.

Practice 2

1. Have students read the directions for the activity and look at the example.

2. Pair Work. Have students take turns asking what is at specific locations.

Extension

Divide the class into groups of three or four. Have students take turns describing their neighborhoods to each other.

Listen to This

Class CD 2, Track 38

Part 1

1. Have students read the directions for the activity.

2. Play or read the conversation. Tell students to listen for what the first person wants to know.

   A: Excuse me. I'm new in town. Can you tell me a little about the neighborhood?
   B: Sure. What do you want to know?
   A: Well, first of all, I'm looking for a bookstore. Is there one around here?
   B: Hmm. Well the nearest one is on Forest Drive, across from the bank.
   A: Forest Drive?
   B: Yeah. The bookstore is between 2nd and 3rd. But it's not very good I'm afraid.
   A: OK. I'll look anyway. And how about places to eat? Can you recommend a good Indian restaurant?
   B: There's one on the corner of 2nd and Pine Street— the Taj Mahal. I go there all the time. It's across from the subway entrance.
   A: On the corner of Second and Pine? OK. Got that. What about if I just want coffee?
   B: You could try the coffee shop on Grove Street, across from the park. It's also across from the gym I go to. It has great coffee and cakes, and the prices are very good.
   A: So, the coffee shop is on Fourth and Grove—across from the gym?
   B: That's right.
   A: How about a hairdresser? I need to get my hair cut.
   B: Try the one on the corner of Grove and 2nd. It's OK.
   A: Great. And how about a Chinese restaurant? Where is that?
   B: There's a great one on Fourth, next to the gym. But it's very small and it's always crowded.

3. Ask volunteers for their answer.

   Answer:
   a little about the neighborhood

Part 2

1. Have students read the directions for the activity and look at the list of places and the map.

2. Play or read the conversation again and tell students to listen for the specific location of each of the places on the list. Tell them to write the places in the correct boxes on the map.

3. Play or read the conversation again for students to check their answers.

4. Ask volunteers for their answers.

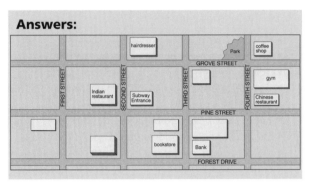

Answers:

Part 3

1. Have students read the directions for the activity.

2. Pair Work. Have students discuss which places the man recommends and put a ✓ next to those places on the map. Play or read the conversation again, if necessary.

Answers:
Taj Mahal Indian restaurant; coffee shop; gym

Let's Talk

Part 1

1. Have students read the directions for the activity, and the example below the map.

2. Pair Work. Have students work with a partner to draw a map of the school neighborhood. Tell them to mark five places they know.

3. Circulate and help as needed.

Part 2

1. Have students read the directions for the activity.

2. Group Work. Have pairs get together in groups of four or six. Have the groups compare their maps and add as many places as they can to their maps.

3. Have groups compare their maps to see which group could label the most things.

Extension

Class Discussion. Have the class talk about places they like to go in the school's neighborhood.

How do I get there?

Student Book page 84

Vocabulary

Introduce these words and phrases to the students:

check: to look at something and make sure it is correct

block: the section of a street between two perpendicular streets

intersection: the place where two streets intersect

go along: move ahead without turning left or right

Prelistening

1. Have students open their books and look at the photograph. Ask:

   • *What are the speakers doing?* (driving somewhere and looking at a map)

2. Pair Work. Read the title of the conversation and the prelistening questions. Have students take turns asking and answering the questions. Help with vocabulary as needed.

4. Class Work. Have pairs share their answers with the class.

Conversation 2

Class CD 2, Track 39

1. With books closed, play the recording or read the conversation.

   Arun: You check the map and I'll drive.
   Kim: OK. Go down this street for about three blocks. You are going to turn at the next intersection.
   Arun: Do I turn right or left?
   Kim: Sorry. Turn left after the drugstore.
   Arun: OK. Now what?
   Kim: Now we go along this street for three blocks. Their building is number 366.
   Arun: There it is. But where can we park the car?
   Kim: There's a parking lot just down the street, across from the supermarket.

2. Ask this comprehension question:

   • *In general, what are the speakers talking about?* (directions to an apartment)

3. Say: *Listen again. This time listen to the details of the conversation.*

4. Play or read the conversation again, pausing for choral repetition. Allow students to write down the information as they listen. Play or read the conversation again, if needed, for students to get all the information.

5. Ask the following questions:

   • *Who is driving?* (Speaker 1)
   • *How many blocks do they go down?* (three)
   • *Where do they turn?* (at the next intersection)
   • *At what place do they turn? Which direction do they turn?* (the drugstore; left)
   • *How many blocks do they go after they turn?* (three)
   • *What is the apartment number?* (366)
   • *Where can they park the car?* (in a parking lot across from the supermarket)

   Elicit responses from various students.

PRONUNCIATION FOCUS

Class CD 2, Track 40

1. Explain what the focus is. Play or read the examples in the book and have students repeat chorally.

   drugstore
   parking lot
   supermarket

2. With books open, play or read the conversation again. Tell students to pay attention to the pronunciation of the compound words.

3. Paired Reading. Have students practice the conversation, switching roles.

Give It a Try

1. Giving directions

Presentation

1. Have students look at the function box and the illustrations. Give them time to read the examples.

2. Model the exchanges and have students repeat chorally.

3. Practice a few exchanges with various students.

Notes

1. In the United States, when people are giving someone directions, people often describe distances in terms of time, for example, *a five-minute walk* or *a twenty-minute drive*.

2. The metric system is not used in the United States. Distances on road signs are in miles. One mile is equal to 1.6 kilometers.

Practice 1

Class CD 2, Track 41

1. Have students read the directions for the activity and look at the illustrations.

2. Play or read the example conversation twice.

   A: Excuse me. Is there a drugstore around here?
   B: Yes, there is. Go up Pine Street to the intersection. Turn left at the corner. It's on Main Street, across from the post office.
   A: Thank you.
   B: No problem.

3. Pair Work. Have students take turns giving directions using one of the four pictures. The partner then says which picture is being described.

Extension

Draw a map on the board. Include several places on the map. Have a student come to the board and hold a piece of chalk to one of the places. He/She then asks another student how to get to another location on the map. As the student gives directions, the first student draws the route to check his/her comprehension and the accuracy of the directions. Erase the route and continue with other pairs.

Practice 2

Class CD 2, Track 42

1. Have students read the directions for the activity and look at the map, the list of places, and the example.

2. Play or read the example conversation twice.

   A: How do I get to the bus stop?
   B: OK. Go along Pine Street to the corner of Oak. Turn right onto Oak and walk two blocks. You can't miss it.

3. Pair Work. Have students take turns asking and giving directions.

4. Have several pairs demonstrate their conversations to the class.

Listen to This

Class CD 2, Track 43

Part 1

1. Have students read the directions for the activity and look at the choices.

2. Play or read the conversation. Tell students to listen for which place the person does *not* ask directions to.

   A: You look lost. Can I help you?

   B: Well, yes, I'm new in town, and I'm looking for somewhere to eat. Where is the nearest cafe?

   A: Let me see. OK. So we're on Union. Just walk up Webb Street until you come to Naples Street. Then take a right. There's a cafe on your left. It's really nice. I often have lunch there.

   B: Great. And what about a drugstore?

   A: Oh, that's easy. Turn left and go down Union until you come to Pine. Then turn right and go up Pine for two blocks. There's a drugstore on the right, on the corner of Green and Pine. I've been there a few times. Their prices are good.

   B: OK. And how about a music store? I want to look at CDs and DVDs.

   A: Sure. You need to go up Webb Street for about three blocks and take a right at Naples. Go down Naples for a couple of blocks and there's a music store on your right. I hear it's good, but I've never been there.

   B: Fantastic. Just one more thing. I hope you don't mind?

   A: Not at all.

   B: Thanks. These shoes are killing me. How can I get to a good shoe store?

   A: Easy. Go down Union for two blocks and then turn right on Pine and go another block or so. There's a shoe store on the corner of Virginia and Pine. I bought these shoes there and they're very comfortable.

   A: Thanks so much. And there is just one more question. I want to go to a good club tonight.

   B: Hmm. I think there's one near here, but I've never been to it. Yes. Go up Webb for two blocks and turn right on Green. There's a club on your right, on the corner of Scott and Green.

   A: Great. Thanks a lot!

3. Ask volunteers for the answers.

   Answer:
   train station

Part 2

1. Have students read the directions for the activity and look at the map.

2. Play or read the conversation again. Tell students to mark on the map the places the person asks directions to and label them.

3. Play the conversation again for students to check their answers.

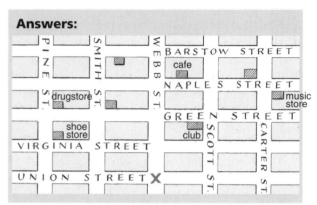

Answers:

Part 3

1. Have students read the directions for the activity.

2. Pair Work. Have students take turns telling each other where they are and then ask for and give directions.

3. Have several groups demonstrate their conversations for the class.

Extension

Have students take turns asking the class to recommend a cafe, a hairdresser, a clothing store, etc. Then have someone from the class give directions to it from the school. Continue with several students.

Person to Person

Part 1

1. Divide the class into pairs and have students decide who will be Student A and who will be Student B. Remind Student B to look at page 112.

2. Have students read the instructions and look at the map.

3. Pair Work. Have Student A ask Student B about the places listed on the map. Encourage Student B to pretend to know about each place, to say if he/she has been there, and if they liked it or not and why. Student A labels each place at the correct location.

4. Circulate and help as needed.

Part 2

1. Have students read the directions for the activity.

2. Pair Work. Have Student B ask Student A about the places listed on the map. Encourage Student A to pretend to know about each place, and to say if he/she has been there and, to say if they liked it or not and why. Student B labels each place at the correct location.

3. Circulate and help as needed.

Part 3

1. Have students read the directions for the activity. Give Student B time to add the places listed onto the map.

2. Pair Work. Have Student A ask Student B how to get to the places listed. Encourage Student B to pretend to know about each place and say if he/she has been there and if they like it or not and why.

3. Circulate and help as needed.

Now Try This

1. Have students read the directions for the activity.

2. Give students time to think of five famous or interesting places in their town. They should write down where each place is and directions for how to get to it from the train or bus station.

3. Pair Work. Have students take turns giving directions to the places on their list.

Could you lend me $20?

Components

Student Book, pages 88–95, 113
Class CD 2, Tracks 44–54
Optional Activities 11.1–11.2,
page 112

Objectives

Functions: Asking to borrow things, declining requests and giving a reason, asking for and giving permission, declining permission and giving a reason

Topics: Everyday activities, formal and informal requests

Structures: *Can…? Could…?*

Pronunciation Focus: Intonation of *Wh-* questions

Listen to This: Listening to people making requests and asking permission

---

Student Book page 88

CONSIDER THIS

1. Have students read the information and the questions. Go over any vocabulary students don't know.

2. Group Work. Divide students into groups of four or five. Have students in each group take turns asking and answering the questions. Help students with vocabulary as needed.

3. Have students talk about borrowing and lending things.

Vocabulary

Introduce these words and phrases to the students:

No problem: used to express that something is OK

broke: not having any money

Prelistening

1. Pair Work. Have students open their books and look at the photograph. Have partners describe what they see to each other. Circulate and help with vocabulary as needed.

2. Class Work. Read the title of the conversation and the prelistening questions. Ask volunteers to answer the questions.

3. Pair Work. Have students take turns asking and answering the questions. Help with vocabulary as needed.

4. Class Work. Ask volunteers to answer the questions. Find out what is the most commonly borrowed item.

Conversation 1

Class CD 2, Track 44

1. With books closed, play the recording or read the conversation.

Ben: Hi, Wade. How are things?
Wade: Pretty good, thanks. How are you?
Ben: I'm fine. By the way, can I borrow your digital camera tonight? I have to take some photos for my class project.
Wade: Sure. No problem.
Ben: Thanks a lot.
Wade: You're welcome.
Ben: Oh, one more thing. Could you lend me $20 until the weekend? I'm broke.
Wade: Sorry, I can't. I'm broke, too!

2. Ask these comprehension questions:

   • *What do you think the relationship between the two speakers is? How do you know?* (They are friends. One is asking to borrow things from the other.)

3. Play or read the conversation again, pausing for choral repetition.

4. Ask the following questions:

- *What does Speaker 1 ask to borrow first?* (Speaker 2's digital camera)
- *Why does he want to borrow it?* (He needs to take photos for a class project.)
- *What is Speaker 2's response?* (Sure. No problem.)
- *What else does Speaker 1 ask to borrow?* ($20)
- *When does he say he will pay Speaker 2 back?* (on the weekend)
- *Can Speaker 2 lend him money? Why not?* (no; He's broke.)

Elicit responses from various students.

5. Paired Reading. Have students read the conversation, switching roles.

Student Book page 89

Give It a Try

1. Asking to borrow things

Presentation

1. Have students look at the function box. Give them time to read the examples.

2. Model the exchanges and have students repeat chorally.

3. Practice a few exchanges with various students.

Notes

1. Review stress of content words in a sentence. On the board, write:

   •
   Can I borrow your camera?

   •
   Would you lend me $20?

   Remind students that the content words are the words that give the important information in a sentence. Have volunteers come to the board and mark the content words in each sentence. Model each sentence and have students repeat.

2. Point out that *Could I borrow your pen?* is a more formal way to ask *Can I borrow your pen?* Also, explain that tone of voice can make a request more polite. Model the questions and have students practice making the requests with different tones of voice to hear the difference.

Practice 1

Class CD 2, Track 45

1. Have students read the directions for the activity and look at the pictures and the examples.

2. Play or read the example conversation twice.

   A: Can I borrow your digital camera?
   B: Sure. No problem. Can you lend me your dictionary?
   A: All right.

3. Pair Work. Have students take turns requesting the items pictured and responding affirmatively to the request. Make sure students use the different question forms from the function box.

4. Have students demonstrate their conversation to the class.

Practice 2

Class CD 2, Track 46

1. Have students read the directions for the activity. Give them time to think of three things they would like to borrow from classmates and have them write the items on the lines.

2. Play or read the example conversation twice.

   A: Do you think I could borrow your book?
   B: Yes, of course.

3. Group Work. Divide the class into groups of three or four. Have students take turns requesting the items and responding affirmatively. Make sure students ask more formally.

4. Have students demonstrate their conversations to the class.

Extension

Ask students about the etiquette of borrowing in their culture. Is it rude to ask to borrow certain things? Are people always expected to return what they borrow? Are people expected to return things within a certain period of time?

2. Declining requests and giving a reason

Review. Point to two students and have one of them ask to borrow something from the other. The other student should respond affirmatively. Quickly go around the class pointing to different pairs and alternating between formal and informal requests.

Presentation

1. Have students look at the function box. Give them time to read the examples.

2. Model the exchanges and have students repeat chorally.

3. Practice a few exchanges with various students.

Notes

1. Review intonation of *Can…?* questions. On the board, write:

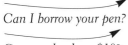

Can I borrow your pen?

Can you lend me $10?

Remind students that the intonation in these questions rises at the end. Mark the intonation in the questions. Model and have students repeat.

2. Explain to students that tone of voice is very important when declining a request. They should sound sincerely sorry when they decline and give their reason for declining. Model the appropriate tone and have students repeat.

Practice 1

Class CD 2, Track 47

1. Have students read the directions for the activity and look at the illustration, the list of requests, and the words in the box. Brainstorm other reasons to decline a request to borrow something.

2. Play or read the example conversation twice.

   A: Can I borrow your pen?
   B: Sorry, but I'm using it.

3. Pair Work. Have students take turns making a request and declining. Encourage students to think of their own reasons for declining the request.

4. Have pairs demonstrate their conversation for the class.

Practice 2

Class CD 2, Track 48

1. Have students read the directions for the activity.

2. Give students time to think of three more requests and write them down.

3. Play or read the example conversation twice.

   A: Do you think I could borrow your laptop?
   B: Sorry, I need it myself.

4. Group Work. Divide the class into groups of three or four. Have students take turns making requests and responding negatively. Make sure students give a reason for declining the request.

5. Have students demonstrate their conversations to the class.

Extension

Divide the class into pairs. Have them write a funny role play of someone requesting something and the other person declining and giving a reason. The person making the request doesn't take *no* for an answer and keeps giving reasons for needing something, while the other person keeps thinking of reasons to decline. Have pairs perform their role plays for the class. Have the class vote on the funniest role play.

Listen to This

Class CD 2, Track 49

Part 1

1. Have students read the directions for the activity and look at the chart.

2. Play or read the conversations. Tell students to listen for what the people want to borrow and number the items.

   1
   A: Oh, that looks nice. Is it new?
   B: Yes, it is. It's the latest model.
   A: It has a nice big screen.
   B: Yes, it does. But it's very light. It only weighs 3 kilos.
   A: Wow. You know, I'm working on an assignment and I wonder if I could borrow it just for tonight?
   B: Umm, actually I will be using it tonight. I have to finish my assignment as well.

2

A: What are you listening to? Music?

B: Actually I'm listening to a Chinese lesson. I'm taking Chinese this semester and we have a test coming up.

A: Oh, I see. Then I suppose you won't be able to lend it to me for the weekend? I'm going away for the weekend and I want to be able to listen to some music on the train.

B: Well, maybe some other time.

3

A: This one is nice. It's very light.

B: Yeah, I love using it. I play much better with it, and I can hit the ball much harder.

A: I'd love to try it some time. Do you think I could borrow it on Saturday afternoon? I'm playing with my cousin.

B: Sure, no problem.

4

A: That looks nice. Is it easy to use?

B: Very easy. And it takes great pictures. You can download them and put them onto your laptop as well.

A: I see. I'm thinking of buying one. Can I borrow yours for a few days to see how easy it is to use?

B: Well, actually I'm using it for the next few days.

A: Oh, OK. No problem.

5

A: Do you use this often?

B: Yes, when the weather is good I ride to school on it.

A: How about on the weekend? Do you use it much then?

B: Not really.

A: Well, do you think I could borrow it on Saturday afternoon?

B: Sure. Just come by and pick it up after lunch.

6

A: I haven't read that. Is it good?

B: Yes, it's terrific.

A: Can I borrow it when you're finished with it?

B: Sure. I'm nearly finished with it. I'll let you have it tomorrow.

A: Thanks a lot.

3. Ask volunteers for their answers.

> **Answers:**
> Going down each column: 1, 4, 6, 5, 3, 2

Part 2

1. Have students read the directions for the activity.

2. Play or read the conversations again and tell students to listen for if the person accepts or refuses the requests.

3. Play or read the conversation again for students to check their answers.

4. Ask volunteers for their answers.

> **Answers:**
> Going down each column: refuse, refuse, accept, accept, accept, refuse

Part 3

1. Have students read the directions for the activity.

2. Pair Work. Have students discuss if they would feel comfortable asking a classmate or a family member to borrow the items.

3. Have students report on their discussions to the class.

Let's Talk

Part 1

1. Have students read the directions for the activity and look at the questions and choices.

2. Pair Work. Have students answer the questions together.

3. Circulate and help as needed.

4. Have students report their answers to the class.

Part 2

1. Have students read the directions for the activity and look at the requests. Give them time to think of reasons to say *no* to each request.

2. Pair Work. Have students take turns requesting each item, refusing, and then giving a reason.

3. Have pairs demonstrate their conversations for the class.

Let's have a party!

Vocabulary

Introduce these words and phrases to the students:

Do you mind if…?: Is it OK if…?

supper: another word for dinner

Prelistening

1. Have students open their books and look at the photograph. Ask:

   - *What do you think the relationship between the two speakers is?* (student and homestay mother)
   - *Where are they?* (in the kitchen)

2. Pair Work. Read the title of the conversation and the prelistening questions. Have students take turns asking and answering the questions.

3. Class Work. Have pairs share their answers with the class.

Conversation 2

Class CD 2, Track 50

1. With books closed, play the recording or read the conversation.

   Patty: When is your birthday, Wade?
   Wade: Actually it's next week. On Thursday.
   Patty: Really? What are your plans?
   Wade: Well, do you mind if I invite a few friends over for a small party?
   Patty: That's fine. How many friends do you want to invite?
   Wade: Maybe five or six.
   Patty: Sure. That's no problem.
   Wade: And is it all right if we use the kitchen and cook a meal?
   Patty: Of course. You can cook supper any time you like!

2. Ask this comprehension question:

   - *In general, what are the speakers talking about?* (Speaker 2 wants to have a small party.)

3. Say: *Listen again. This time listen to the details of the conversation.*

4. Play or read the conversation again, pausing for choral repetition. Allow students to write down the information as they listen. Play or read the conversation again, if needed, for students to get all the information.

5. Ask the following questions:

   - *When is Speaker 2's birthday?* (next Thursday)
   - *What are his plans?* (He wants to invite a few friends over.)
   - *How many friends does he want to invite?* (five or six)
   - *What else does Speaker 2 ask to do?* (use the kitchen and cook a meal)
   - *Does Speaker 1 accept or refuse the request?* (She accepts.)

   Elicit responses from various students.

PRONUNCIATION FOCUS

Class CD 2, Track 51

1. Explain what the focus is. Play or read the examples in the book and have students repeat chorally.

   When is your birthday?
   What are your plans?

2. With books open, play or read the conversation again. Tell students to pay attention to the intonation in the questions.

3. Paired Reading. Have students practice the conversation, switching roles.

Give It a Try

1. Asking for and giving permission

Presentation

1. Have students look at the function box. Give them time to read the examples.

2. Model the exchanges and have students repeat chorally.

3. Practice a few exchanges with various students.

Practice 1

Class CD 2, Track 52

1. Have students read the directions for the activity and look at the illustration and the list of requests. Give students time to think of their own request.

2. Play or read the example conversation twice.

   A: Is it OK if I invite my friends over next week?
   B: Sure. No problem.

3. Pair Work. Have students take turns asking permission to do the things on the list in an informal way. Answers should be affirmative.

4. Have pairs demonstrate for the class.

Practice 2

1. Have students read the directions for the activity.

2. Put the class in different pairs than in Practice 1.

3. Pair Work. Have students take turns asking permission to do the things on the list in a formal way. Answers should be affirmative.

4. Have pairs demonstrate for the class.

Extension

Ask the class about being a good dinner guest or houseguest in their culture. Does the guest bring a gift? Are there things the guest shouldn't ask permission to do?

2. Declining permission and giving a reason

Presentation

1. Have students look at the function box. Give them time to read the examples.

2. Model the exchanges and have students repeat chorally.

3. Practice a few exchanges with various students.

Notes

1. Remind students that the proper tone is very important when refusing someone permission. Explain that it is polite to sound sincerely sorry that you cannot give permission. Model responses and have students repeat.

2. Explain the term *white lie*. Tell students that it is a small untruthful statement that people say when they don't want to tell the truth because telling the truth would hurt someone's feelings or make you feel uncomfortable. Have the class think of examples of situations where someone would tell a white lie and examples of actual white lies.

Practice 1

Class CD 2, Track 53

1. Have students read the directions for the activity and look at the list of requests and the phrases in the box. Brainstorm other reasons to decline a request.

2. Play or read the example conversation twice.

   A: Do you mind if I watch TV?
   B: Well, maybe later if you don't mind.

3. Pair Work. Have students take turns making a request from the list, declining it, and giving a reason.

Practice 2

1. Have students read the directions for the activity.

2. Give students time to think of three more requests a houseguest might make.

3. Pair Work. Have students take turns making requests and declining them.

Listen to This

Class CD 2, Track 54

Part 1

1. Have students read the directions for the activity and look at the choices and the illustrations.

2. Play or read the conversations. Tell students to listen for where the speakers are.

1

A: I thought I would listen to the sports. Can I turn it on? Is that OK with you?

B: Umm, you know, I've got a bit of a headache and I'm trying to rest. Would you mind listening to it later?

A: Not at all. Can I get you something for your headache—maybe some aspirin and some tea with lemon?

B: That would be nice, thanks.

2

A: I really feel like a cup of coffee. Can I use the coffeemaker?

B: Do you know how to use it?

A: I think so.

B: All right. Actually I think I'll have one, too.

A: Do you like it with milk and sugar?

B: Yes, thank you.

3

A: Oh gosh, I forgot to call home. I said I would call about now. Is that OK with you?

B: Of course. You can make your call from the phone in the kitchen. It's nice and quiet there.

A: Thanks so much.

4

A: Do you mind if I watch the news? I want to find out what's happening at home and I haven't had a chance to read the newspaper today.

B: Not at all. I'll just turn off the radio.

A: Thanks. I only want to catch the headlines.

5

A: I need to get some clothes ready for the weekend. Is it OK if I use the iron for a while?

B: Yes, it's in the kitchen. Look in the cupboard on the left.

A: OK. I see it. Thanks.

3. Ask volunteers for the answers.

> **Answer:**
> a friend's house

Part 2

1. Have students read the directions for the activity.

2. Play or read the conversations again. Tell students to put a ✓ next to the illustrations of the requests he/she agrees to.

3. Play the conversation again for students to check their answers.

> **Answers:**
> coffee maker, phone, TV, iron

Person to Person

Part 1

1. Divide the class into pairs and have students decide who will be Student A and who will be Student B. Remind Student B to look at page 113.

2. Have students read the directions and look at the pictures of the items. Brainstorm reasons to borrow each item and reasons to refuse to lend them.

3. Pair Work. Have Student A ask to borrow the three items listed. Student B agrees to lend one item but must refuse to lend the other items and must give reasons why he/she is refusing.

4. Circulate and help as needed.

Part 2

1. Have students read the instructions and look at the illustration. Brainstorm reasons to ask permission to do those things and reasons to not agree.

2. Pair Work. Have Student B ask permission to do three things. Student A agrees to one of the requests but must refuse permission for the two other things and give reasons.

Part 3

1. Have students read the directions for the activity.

2. Pair Work. Have Student A and Student B reverse roles and do Part 2 again.

Now Try This

1. Have students read the directions.

2. Have the class brainstorm excuses for saying *no* to requests to borrow money, a tennis racket, and a magazine.

Extension

Have students tell the class about times when they had to refuse a request and why they refused. Ask if they have ever told a *white lie* to give an excuse.

Unit 12 — How was your year?

Components

Student Book, pages 96–103
Class CD 2, Tracks 55–64
Optional Activities 12.1–12.2,
page 113

Objectives

Functions: Talking about past experiences, talking about future plans, talking about wants

Topics: Future plans, wants

Structures: *Be going to*, time phrases, past tense, *Wh-* questions

Pronunciation Focus: Pronunciation of *want to*

Listen to This: Listening to people's future plans

Student Book page 96

CONSIDER THIS

1. Have students read the information and the question. Go over any vocabulary students don't know.

2. Group Work. Divide students into groups of four or five. Have students in each group take turns talking about New Year's celebrations. Help students with vocabulary as needed.

3. Ask volunteers to share their experiences with the class.

Vocabulary

Introduce these words and phrases to the students:

And you?: Used to ask someone the same question they have just asked you

ski slopes: the hills that someone skis down

even (better): used to emphasize how much (better) something is

Prelistening

1. Pair Work. Have students open their books and look at the photograph. Have partners describe what they see to each other. Circulate and help with vocabulary as needed.

2. Class Work. Read the title of the conversation and the prelistening questions. Ask volunteers to answer the questions.

3. Pair Work. Have students take turns asking and answering the questions. Help with vocabulary as needed.

4. Class Work. Ask volunteers to answer the questions.

Conversation 1

Class CD 2, Track 55

1. With books closed, play the recording or read the conversation.

    Yi-lin: So did you have a good year, Andy?
    Andy: Yeah, it was pretty good, thanks. How about you?
    Yi-lin: I had a good year, too.
    Andy: Did you do anything special this year?
    Yi-lin: Well, I took a judo class. That was fun. And you?
    Andy: I went to Canada for a vacation. It was terrific.
    Yi-lin: What was your best experience in Canada?
    Andy: On the ski slopes. I went skiing every day. I really enjoyed it.
    Yi-lin: That's great. And I hope next year is even better.

2. Ask these comprehension questions:

    • *Do the speakers see each other often? How do you know?* (no; They are talking about the things they did during the last year.)

3. Play or read the conversation again, pausing for choral repetition.

4. Ask the following questions:

   - *Did the speakers have a good year?* (yes)
   - *What special thing did Speaker 1 do?* (She took a judo class.)
   - *What special thing did Speaker 2 do?* (He went to Canada for vacation.)
   - *Was it a good vacation?* (yes)
   - *What was Speaker 2's best experience in Canada?* (skiing every day)

   Elicit responses from various students.

5. Paired Reading. Have students read the conversation, switching roles.

Student Book page 97

Give It a Try

1. Talking about past experiences (1)

Presentation

1. Have students look at the function box. Give them time to read the examples.

2. Model the exchanges and have students repeat chorally.

3. Practice a few exchanges with various students.

Notes

1. Review intonation of *Did you…?* questions. On the board, write:

   Did you have a good year?

   Did you do anything interesting?

   Remind students that the intonation in these questions rises at the end. Mark the intonation in the questions. Model and have students repeat.

2. Tell students that in the United States New Year's Eve (December 31) is usually celebrated with parties with family and friends. People stay up and yell *Happy New Year!* at midnight. People also make New Year resolutions. These are promises you make to yourself to do something better in the coming year. For example, people make resolutions to exercise more, stop smoking, or eat healthier foods.

3. This would be a good time to review irregular past tense verbs. Make a list of common irregular verbs on the board and have students say the past tense. Write the past tense of each verb on the board and have students keep a list in their notebooks. They should add to their list throughout the Unit.

Practice 1

Class CD 2, Track 56

1. Have students read the directions for the activity and look at the chart.

2. Give students time to think about what they did this year and check them.

3. Play or read the example twice.

   A: Did you have a good year?
   B: It was pretty good, thanks.
   A: Did you do anything interesting?
   B: Yes, I took a judo class. Did you do anything interesting?
   A: No, not really.

4. Pair Work. Have students take turns saying the things they did during the year and asking follow-up questions.

5. Have students demonstrate their conversation to the class.

Practice 2

1. Have students read the directions for the activity and look at the example.

2. Pair Work. Have students pair off with a different partner from Practice 1. Have them take turns telling each other something interesting their first partner did during the year.

3. Have students demonstrate their conversations to the class.

Extension

Have students discuss what they like to do to celebrate the New Year.

2. Talking about past experiences (2)

Review. Quickly review past tense of irregular verbs. Say a verb in the present tense. Point to a student and have them say the past tense. Move rapidly around the classroom.

Note

Review irregular comparatives and superlatives. On the board, write:

My vacation this year was good.

My vacation last year was better.

My vacation two years ago was the best.

Model the sentences and have students repeat. Have volunteers say the above sentences again, substituting with *bad, worse,* and *the worst.*

Presentation

1. Have students look at the function box. Give them time to read the examples.

2. Model the exchanges and have students repeat chorally.

3. Practice a few exchanges with various students.

Practice

Class CD 2, Track 57

1. Have students read the directions for the activity and look at the illustrations and the chart. Have students say what is happening in each picture.

2. Give students time to fill in the chart with information about their experiences in the past year.

3. Play or read the example conversation twice.

    A: Did you do anything special?
    B: Yes. I got a new job. And you? What was your best experience?
    A: My trip to the US—I went to San Francisco for a week.
    B: Oh, that sounds great!

4. Pair Work. Have students take turns asking and answering questions about their experiences in the last year.

5. Have students report on their partner's activities to the class.

Extension

Do the Practice again. This time, have students answer the questions in the chart with made-up experiences. Encourage students to think of experiences that are funny, imaginative, and interesting.

Listen to This

Class CD 2, Track 58

Part 1

1. Have students read the directions for the activity and look at the chart and the experiences listed in the first column.

2. Play or read the conversations. Tell students to listen for what the people did and put the number of the dialog next to the correct activity.

1
A: Did you have a good year, Taylor?
B: Very good, thanks. Look at this.
A: An engagement ring. Fantastic! I didn't know you were engaged.
B: Yes, I got engaged last month. I met my fiance when I was on vacation last summer. We're planning to get married next year.
A: Congratulations! That's wonderful news.

2
A: How was school this year, Pei-ling?
B: Oh, so-so.
A: Only so-so? How come?
B: Yes, you know I am very interested in languages, and this year I decided to try to learn German. So I took a German class at night school.
A: Was it difficult?
B: Difficult and very boring. So I dropped it after one month.

3
A: So are you still living near school, Carlos?
B: No, we had to move. So now we're staying out near the airport.
A: Oh. So what's it like out there?
B: Not very nice actually. We hear a lot of aircraft noise, and it takes a long time to get into town.
A: That's too bad. I hate getting stuck in traffic.
B: Tell me about it!

4

A: How was your year, Devi? Did you enjoy your classes at City College?

B: Actually, I didn't complete the year there. I was taking a computer course but I decided I wanted to study business instead, so I changed to a new school—New World Business College.

A: Really? I don't know that school. How was it?

B: Very good. I learned a lot.

5

A: So did you have a good year, Fadi?

B: Not bad, thanks. The best thing was my trip last summer.

A: Where did you go?

B: Thailand and Vietnam.

A: Did you enjoy it?

B: Yeah, it was great.

6

A: Did you have an interesting year, Chloe?

B: I guess it was interesting. But not what I expected.

A: Really?

B: Yeah, I bought a new car.

A: Well, that sounds interesting.

B: Not really. I only had it for a month and someone stole it.

A: No way! That's terrible!

3. Ask volunteers for their answers.

> **Answers:**
> 5, 6, 1, 3, 4, 2

Part 2

1. Have students read the directions for the activity and look at the second column in the chart.

2. Play or read the conversations again and tell students to listen for if the person has positive or negative feelings.

3. Play or read the conversation again for students to check their answers.

4. Ask volunteers for their answers.

> **Answers:**
> positive; negative; positive; negative; positive; negative

Part 3

1. Have students read the directions for the activity.

2. Pair Work. Have students discuss which person had the best year and who had the worst. Play or read the conversations again, if necessary. Have students discuss their own lives and decide who had the better year.

3. Have students report on their discussion to the class.

Let's Talk

Part 1

1. Have students read the directions for the activity and look at the chart.

2. Give students time to check the things they did and try to remember the details of each activity.

3. Circulate and help as needed.

Part 2

1. Have students read the directions for the activity and look at the follow-up questions.

2. Pair Work. Have students take turns asking about their partner's activities and writing the answers to the follow-up questions in the chart.

Part 3

1. Have students read the directions for the activity.

2. Have students report on the things they and their partners had in common. Encourage the class to ask follow-up questions to the person reporting.

What are your plans?

Student Book page 100

Vocabulary

Introduce these words and phrases to the students:

lots: many

open a business: to start a business that you are the owner of

graduate: to successfully complete a course of study

Prelistening

1. Have students open their books and look at the photograph. Ask:

   - *Where are the speakers?* (in a college cafeteria or break room)
   - *What are they doing?* (eating snacks, drinking, and talking)

2. Pair Work. Read the title of the conversation and the prelistening question. Have students take turns asking and answering the question.

3. Class Work. Have pairs share their answers with the class.

Conversation 2

Class CD 2, Track 59

1. With books closed, play the recording or read the conversation.

   Yi-lin: So what are your plans for next year, Rina? Are you going to get a job?
   Rina: No, I'm going to go to college.
   Yi-lin: Great. What school are you going to go to?
   Rina: I want to go to City College. Lots of my friends are going there.
   Yi-lin: Oh. So what do you want to study?
   Rina: I want to study business.
   Yi-lin: That's interesting.
   Rina: Yeah, I want to open a business after I graduate.
   Yi-lin: Well, good luck.

2. Ask this comprehension question:

   - *In general, what are the speakers talking about?* (plans for next year)

3. Say: *Listen again. This time listen to the details of the conversation.*

4. Play or read the conversation again, pausing for choral repetition. Allow students to write down the information as they listen. Play or read the conversation again, if needed, for students to get all the information.

5. Ask the following questions:

   - *What is Speaker 2 going to do next year?* (go to college)
   - *What college will she go to?* (City College)
   - *What is one reason she is going there?* (lots of her friends are going there)
   - *What does Speaker 2 want to study?* (business)
   - *What does Speaker 2 want to do after she graduates?* (open a business)

   Elicit responses from various students.

PRONUNCIATION FOCUS
Class CD 2, Track 60

1. Explain what the focus is. Play or read the examples in the book and have students repeat chorally.

   I want to go to City College.
   What do you want to study?
   I want to study business.

2. With books open, play or read the conversation again. Tell students to pay attention to the pronunciation of *want to*.

3. Paired Reading. Have students practice the conversation, switching roles.

Give It a Try

1. Talking about future plans

Presentation

1. Have students look at the function box. Give them time to read the examples.

2. Model the exchanges and have students repeat chorally.

3. Practice a few exchanges with various students.

Notes

1. Explain the difference between *will* and be *going to*. Tell students that *will* and *be going to* can both be used to express a prediction.

   It will be sunny tomorrow.

   It's going to be sunny tomorrow.

   Only *will* is used to express willingness to do something.

   I will help you wash the dishes.

   Only *be going to* is used to express a prior plan, which is why it is used in the statements in the function box.

   I'm going to visit London next year.

   She's going to study medicine.

2. Review intonation of *What…?* questions. On the board, write:

   What are you going to do next year?

   What are you going to study in college?

   Remind students that the intonation in these questions falls at the end. Mark the intonation in the questions. Model and have students repeat.

3. Point out to students that *going to* is often pronounced /gonna/ in spoken conversation but is never spelled that way in written language.

Practice 1

Class CD 2, Track 61

1. Have students read the directions for the activity and look at the chart and the words and phrases in the box.

2. Give students time to fill in the chart with their information about future plans and the reasons for those plans.

3. Play or read the example conversation twice.

   A: What are you going to do next year?
   B: I'm going to get a job.
   A: Why?
   B: I need to make some money. What are you going to do?
   A: I'm going to go on vacation.

4. Pair Work. Have students compare their answers in the chart.

Practice 2

1. Have students read the directions for the activity and look at the example.

2. Put the class in different pairs than in Practice 1.

3. Pair Work. Have students take turns telling their new partner about their first partner's future plans.

4. Have students report their first partner's plans to the class. Encourage the class to ask follow-up questions.

2. Talking about wants

Presentation

1. Have students look at the function box. Give them time to read the examples.

2. Model the exchanges and have students repeat chorally.

3. Practice a few exchanges with various students.

Note

Point out to students that *want to* is often pronounced /wanna/ in spoken conversation but is never spelled that way in written language.

Practice 1

Class CD 2, Track 62

1. Have students read the directions for the activity and look at the list of plans and the example conversation.

2. Play or read the example conversation twice.

   A: What do you want to do?
   B: Well, I want to get a job.
   A: Do you want to travel?
   B: Yes, I do! What about you?

3. Give students time to check the things they want to do.

4. Pair Work. Have students take turns asking and answering questions about their future plans and asking follow-up questions.

5. Have students report on their partner's future plans to the class.

Practice 2

Class CD 2, Track 63

1. Have students read the directions for the activity and look at the chart.

2. Play or read the example conversation twice.

   A: What place do you want to visit sometime?
   B: I want to visit South Africa.

3. Give students time to answer the questions in the chart.

4. Pair Work. Have students take turns asking and answering the questions in the chart.

5. Have pairs demonstrate their conversation for the class.

Listen to This

Class CD 2, Track 64

Part 1

1. Have students read the directions for the activity and look at the chart.

2. Play or read the conversation. Tell students to listen for what Robert is planning to do.

   A: So, what are your plans for next year, Robert? And are you still planing to learn Spanish?
   R: Maybe not. I think I might try Portuguese instead.
   A: Why Portuguese?
   R: I'm thinking of going to South America toward the end of the year. I'd like to live in Brazil for a couple of years.
   A: Are you just going to travel around Brazil and take a long vacation?
   R: I can't afford to do that. I want to get a job in a school there and teach English for a couple of years. I need to save some money to pay off my school loan.
   A: Wow! That sounds interesting.
   R: I also want to take a photography class.
   A: A photography class?
   R: Yes. Before I go to Brazil I want to take a class. Then when I'm in Brazil, maybe I can take photos for travel magazines. I hear you can make pretty good money that way.
   A: Well, it sounds like you're going to have a busy year. Good luck!
   R: Thanks.

3. Ask volunteers for the answers.

Answers:
teach English; take a photography class

Part 2

1. Have students read the directions for the activity.

2. Play or read the conversation again. Tell students to write the reasons why or why not Robert does or does not want to do each thing.

3. Play the conversation again for students to check their answers.

> **Answers:**
> wants to live in Brazil; save money to pay off his student loan; take photos for travel magazines

Practice 3

1. Have students read the directions for the activity.

2. Pair Work. Have students discuss if they want to do any of the things mentioned in the conversation.

Student Book page 103

Person to Person

Part 1

1. Have students read the instructions and look at the list of questions. Brainstorm follow-up questions for each question.

2. Pair Work. Have Student A interview Student B and take notes of the answers. Make sure they ask follow-up questions and get as many details as possible.

3. Circulate and help as needed.

Part 2

1. Have students read the instructions.

2. Pair Work. Have Student B interview Student A and take notes of the answers. Make sure they ask follow-up questions and get as many details as possible.

3. Circulate and help as needed.

Part 3

1. Have students read the directions for the activity and look at the example questions.

2. Group Work. Have two pairs get together and share their information. Have the group answer the Part 3 questions.

Now Try This

1. Have students remain in their groups and read the instructions for the activity.

2. Group Work. Have students plan a five-day vacation for a visitor to their country.

3. Have someone from each group describe the vacation they planned. Have the class vote on who planned the best vacation.

Extension

Divide the class into new pairs. Have them imagine that one person recommended a five-day vacation and the other person just returned from it. Role-play the conversation about where you went, how long you stayed, what you did, etc. Have several groups demonstrate for the class.

Student Book page 104

Listen to This Unit 10

Class CD 2, Track 65

Part 1

1. Have students read the directions and look at the map.

2. Play or read the conversations.

1
A: Where can I find a supermarket?
B: Go up Ford Street to the first corner and turn right onto Wilson Street. It's the second building on your right.
A: Thanks.

2
A: I'm looking for a mailbox. Is there one around here?
B: Yes, there is one just down the street on the corner of Ford and Wilson. It's next to the drugstore.

3
A: I'm looking for a coffee shop. Do you know a good one around here?
B: Sure. Go up Ford for a block and turn left. There's one about halfway down the first block, across from the bank.

4
A: Where's the subway entrance, please?
B: Oh, go up Ford to the first corner and turn right. There's one on the other side of the road, across from the supermarket.

5
A: I need to see a dentist. Do you know where I can find one?
B: A dentist. Let me see. Oh yes, there's one on Wilson Street. Go down Ford and turn left onto Wilson. There's one about a block down on the left-hand side, across from the hotel.

6
A: Where can I buy some good magazines?
B: There's a very good bookstore not far from here. It's on Wilson. Turn right at the corner of Wilson and Ford. There's one on the corner, across from the bank.

3. Have students write the number of the conversation in the correct circle.

4. Play or read the conversations again for students to check their answers.

Answers:

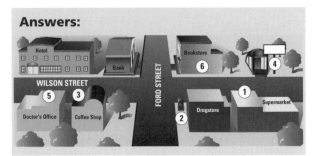

Part 2

1. Pair Work. Have students look at their maps and ask and answer questions about the locations of the places.

2. Ask several students for their answers.

Give It a Try

1. Have students read the directions and look at the list of places and questions.

2. Pair Work. Have students take turns asking the questions and answering them.

3. Have several pairs demonstrate for the class.

Listen to This Unit 11

Class CD 2, Track 66

Part 1

1. Have students read the directions and look at the chart.

2. Play or read the conversations. Have students put a ✓ under *Permission* or *Borrow*.

1
A: Oh, there's a great TV program on in few minutes. Do you mind if I turn on the TV?
B: Well actually, I'm trying to study for a test.
A: Oh, never mind.

2
A: It's awfully hot in here. Can I open the window?
B: It is hot. Yeah, please do.
A: Thanks.

3

A: Do you mind lending me this book? I'd like to read it. I hear it's really good.

B: Yeah, help yourself.

A: Thanks.

4

A: Can I use your car tonight? I have a date.

B: Umm, actually I need it myself tonight. I have a date, too.

A: Oh, too bad.

3. Play or read the conversations again for students to check their answers.

4. Ask several students for the answers.

> **Answers:**
> 1. permission
> 2. permission
> 3. borrow
> 4. borrow

Student Book page 105

Part 2

1. Have students read the directions.

2. Play or read the conversations again. Have students put a ✓ under Agree or Doesn't agree.

> **Answers:**
> 1. doesn't agree
> 2. agrees
> 3. agrees
> 4. doesn't agree

Give It a Try

1. Have students read the directions and look at the list of requests.

2 Pair Work. Have students take turns asking to borrow things, saying *no*, and then giving a reason.

3. Have several pairs demonstrate one of their conversations for the class.

Listen to This Unit 12

Class CD 2, Track 67

1. Have students read the directions and look at the statements.

2. Play or read the conversation.

A: What are you going to do next summer, Jo?

J: I'm going to go to Australia.

A: Australia. Wow! What are you going to do there?

J: I'm going to travel and I'm also going to work a little to help pay for the trip.

A: Really? What kind of work are you going to do?

J: Oh, anything I can find. Maybe picking fruit or working in a cafe.

A: Great. Are you going to travel with a friend?

J: No, I'm going on my own. But I'm sure I will meet people there.

A: Where are you going to stay?

J: I'm going to stay in hostels.

A: That sounds good. And how long are you going to be away?

J: For about six months.

A: Terrific. I wish I could go with you!

3. Have students check whether each statement is true or false.

4. Play or read the conversation again for students to check their answers.

5. Ask several students for their answers.

> **Answers:**
> 1. true
> 2. false
> 3. false
> 4. true
> 5. false

Give It a Try

1. Have students read the directions and look at the list of question prompts. Give them time to formulate the questions, think of follow-up questions, and add their own idea.

2. Group Work. Have students discuss what they want to do in the future. Make sure students ask each other follow-up questions.

3. Group Work. Have students discuss what they will do to achieve their plans.

4. Have a student from each group report on their group's discussion.

Optional Activities Teacher's Notes

Optional Activity 1.1

Name Game, *page 114*

Preparation: Make one copy of Optional Activity 1.1 for each student.

Procedure: Arrange students into pairs. Distribute one copy of the handout to each student. Ask pairs to read and match the proper names and nicknames. Don't be surprised if students need a lot of help when matching the names. When eliciting the answers, it helps to model the pronunciation of the proper names, with an emphasis on the syllable that translates into the nickname.

Ask pairs to practice the short interaction and test their memories.

In small groups, students discuss the questions.

Answers:

1. C
2. H
3. E
4. J
5. B
6. G
7. I
8. A
9. K
10. F
11. D

Optional Activity 1.2

Hidden Dialog, *page 115*

Preparation: Make one copy of Optional Activity 1.2 for each student.

Procedure: Arrange students into groups of three. Distribute one copy of the handout to each student. Students work together and use the grid to find the missing pieces of dialog. Each line of dialog starts with a numbered box on the grid. Students must move one square up/down/sideways or diagonally to find the next words in the line. Students complete the missing words in the lines of dialog below the grid. Check answers with the class.

Students use their own ideas to adapt or continue the conversation between the three friends.

Answers:

Example: 1. Ben: Hi, Yang. How are you today?

2. Yang: Fine thanks, Ben. How are you?
3. Ben: Fine. Who's that girl?
4. Yang: She's my neighbor, Tina.
5. Ben: She's really cute.

6. Yang: Do you want to meet her?
7. Ben: I sure do.
8. Yang: Tina, this is my classmate, Ben.
9. Tina: Hi, Ben. It's nice to meet you.
10. Ben: *(Possible answer)* Nice to meet you, too.

Optional Activity 2.1

Word Jumble, *page 116*

Preparation: Make one copy of Optional Activity 2.1 for each student.

Procedure: Arrange students into pairs. Distribute one copy of the handout to each student.

Together, students unjumble the vocabulary items (clothing & accessories).

Students match the clues and write the words from Part 1.

When the answers are correct the mystery word runs down the middle.

Answers:

Part 1

1. sweater
2. suit
3. socks
4. rings
5. cell phone
6. cap
7. T-shirt
8. sunglasses
9. umbrella
10. watch
11. sneakers

Part 2

1.   U M **B** R E L L A
2.   C **A** P
3.   W A **T** C H
4. C E L L   P **H** O N E
5.   T-S H **I** R T
6.   S **N** E A K E R S
7.   S U N **G** L A S S E S
8.   S O C K **S**
9.   S **U** I T
10.   R **I** N G S
11. S W E A T E **R**

Part 3

bathing suit

Optional Activity 2.2

Picture Dictation, *page 117*

Preparation: Make one copy of Optional Activity 2.2 for each student.

Procedure: Arrange students into pairs. Distribute one copy of the handout to each student.

Students work together to label all the items on the handout (for example, desk, drawer, computer, lamp). Confirm answers with class.

Individually, students choose six items and draw them in the first picture.

Students describe the placement of their six items to their partners, who listen and draw the items into the second picture. The listener can ask questions if a description is not clear but cannot see their partner's drawing. When all six items have been described, students compare the pictures from the descriptions.

Students switch roles and repeat Part 3.

Additional Practice: Students work with new partners and play Spot the Difference describing their first partner's items.

Optional Activity 3.1

Do you know Student X and Student Y? *page 118*

Preparation: Make as many copies as necessary of Optional Activity 3.1, which consists of ten cards. Prepare one card for each student.

Procedure: Prepare students for the activity. Write the following categories on the board: *name, age, birthday, height, weight, nationality,* and *interests.*

In pairs, students discuss the questions they would ask to find out this information about a third person.

Elicit answers:

Name:	What is his/her name?
Age:	How old is he/she?
Birthday:	When is his/her birthday?
Height:	How tall is he/she?
Weight:	How much does he/she weigh?
Nationality:	What is his/her nationality?
Interests:	What are his/her interests?

Review questions as a class.

Explain the activity scenario to the students by saying:

You have received an incomplete information card for a new student. It is very important that you complete the information before the student arrives. People in the class have different pieces of information about your guest. Ask each other questions to complete the information on your card.

Distribute one card to each student making certain there are at least the five Student X and Student Y cards in circulation.

Students ask each other questions and complete the information on their card. When asked for information, students can only share the information that is printed on their card. Students must have access to information on at least five specific character cards (i.e., Student X or Student Y).

When students have completed their cards, they compare their information in pairs.

Additional Practice: In X/Y pairs, students role-play a meeting between Student X and Student Y.

Answers:

Student X

George Yip
32, March 23rd
180 cm, 80 kg
American
Baseball & Travel

Student Y

Eva King
24, October 7th
160 cm, 58 kg
German
Tennis & Fashion

Optional Activity 3.2

We're a family! *page 119*

Preparation: Make one copy of Optional Activity 3.2 for each student.

Procedure: Arrange students into groups of five students. Distribute one copy of the handout to each student. Students work in groups to complete Part 1 with family/relationship vocabulary. Elicit answers from the class.

Groups imagine that they are all members of the same family. Students discuss the questions and create a profile/description for each family member. Students note down information on the chart in preparation for presenting their family.

Groups take turns presenting the members of their new family to the class.

Answers:

This is a personalization activity with no specific answers. The amount and depth of information created will depend on the level of the students.

Optional Activity 4.1

Observation, *page 120*

Preparation: Make one copy of Optional Activity 4.1 for each student.

Procedure: Arrange students into pairs. Distribute one copy of Optional Activity 4.1 to each student. Make sure students don't look at the handout before you tell them to.

For just one minute, students study the picture at the top of the handout. After one minute, students fold the sheet so they cannot see the picture.

Individually, and working from memory, students have three minutes to answer the questions.

Still working from memory, pairs compare and discuss their answers.

Students look at the picture to check their answers and add up their scores. Scores can be used to rate their level of observation.

Answers:

1. a woman
2. a teenage boy
3. eating an ice cream cone
4. a briefcase and an umbrella
5. a T-shirt, a jacket, jeans, boots, cap, and sunglasses
6. the woman
7. It is short, dark, and straight.
8. his watch
9. the woman
10. the girl
11. a flower
12. the man

Additional Practice: Groups of four students role-play the people waiting in line and start polite conversations with each other. They can discuss things like the weather, general observations, likes and dislikes, and why they are waiting for the bus.

Optional Activity 4.2

Market Day, *page 121*

Preparation: Make one copy of Optional Activity 4.2, which consists of *Student A* and *Student B*, for each pair of students. Cut the copies in two.

Procedure: Divide the class into two groups—A and B. Distribute *Student A* to half the class and *Student B* to the other half.

Review useful vocabulary with the class:

colors/light/dark

beautiful/pretty/fabulous/cool

comfortable/warm/stylish/soft

cheap/expensive/affordable

In pairs (AA/BB), students discuss and complete descriptions of the items they have for sale.

Review useful expressions for buying items with the class:

Do you have a/an _____ for sale?

How much is it/are they?

That's expensive/reasonable/cheap.

In large groups or as whole class, students interact to sell four items and buy four items from at least four classmates. The activity ends with a time limit or when everyone has completed the activity.

Lead class feedback on what people bought, why, and how much they paid. Ask students to add up how much money they spent and how much they made in sales.

Optional Activity 5.1

Ben's Day, *page 122*

Preparation: Make one copy of Optional Activity 5.1, which consists of *Student A* and *Student B*, for each pair of students. Cut the copies in two.

Procedure: Divide the class into two groups—A and B. Distribute *Student A* to half the class and *Student B* to the other half.

In pairs (AA/BB), students discuss the missing information and agree on the questions they need to ask to complete the text, i.e., questions for names, occupations, relationships, times, and daily routines.

Arrange students into AB pairs and remind them not to show their text to their partner. Students take turns asking questions and completing the text with the information from their partner.

When the students have both completed the text, they should read it together and compare answers.

Answers:

Ben is (Ex.) **34**-years-old. He lives in **Chicago** and is married to **Sung-yi**. They have **two** children, a son, **Ty** who is **seven**-years-old and a daughter, **May**, who is **five**-years-old. Ben is a **baker**. He likes his job very much, but he has an unusual daily routine. Ben gets up at **3 A.M.** He leaves home at **3:25 A.M.** and walks to the bakery. He has breakfast at the bakery at **3:45 A.M.** and starts baking for the day at **4 A.M.** The bakery opens at **7 A.M.** It is very busy. Around **8:15 A.M.** Ben has lunch and at **9 A.M.**, he cleans the kitchen and starts preparing for the next day. He finishes work at **1:30 P.M.** and gets home at **2 P.M.** He eats a big dinner with his wife at **2:10 P.M.** and they talk about the day. At **3 P.M.**, he leaves home to meet Ty and May at their school and they all walk home together. Ben plays with his children until the children's dinner time at **5 P.M.** Ben likes to sit with them and have a cup of tea. At **6 P.M.**, he watches the news on TV. After the news, he kisses his wife and children good night, and he goes to bed at 8:15 P.M.

Additional Practice: Discuss the following questions in small groups.

1. Is Ben an early bird or a night owl?
2. What are some good things and bad things about Ben's day?
3. Would you like to have Ben's day? Why? Why not?
4. Do you have any unusual routines?

Optional Activity 5.2

Day Trip, *page 123*

Preparation: Make one copy of Optional Activity 5.2, which consists of *Student A* and *Student B*, for each pair of students. Cut the copies in two.

Procedure: Arrange students into pairs. Distribute *Student A* to one student and *Student B* to the other.

Pairs ask each other questions and complete the missing information about the schedules and prices of different tourist attractions.

When the information is completed, students discuss and agree on an itinerary for their day trip.

Answers:

Student A missing information:

$10.00
Mon., Wed., Thurs., Fri., 12-5 P.M.
Sun.-Thurs. 11:30 A.M.-9 P.M.
May 1-October 15: Daily 10 A.M.-6 P.M.
Free
$25.00-$75.00
2:30, 4:45, 7:00
November-May: Tues.-Sun. 9 A.M.-5 P.M.

Student B missing information:

Tues.-Sun., 11 A.M.-5 P.M.
$6.50
Daily 8 A.M.-4 P.M.
Fri. & Sat. 11:30 A.M.-7 P.M.
$5.00
$15.00
Open 24 hours
Daily (except Tues.), 8 P.M.
$12.00
10 A.M. & 1 P.M.

Additional Practice: Students explain and discuss their itineraries with other partners.

Optional Activity 6.1

Weekend Plans, *page 124*

Preparation: Make one copy of Optional Activity 6.1 for each student.

Procedure: Elicit some activities that students like and don't like to do on weekends. Distribute one copy of the handout to each student.

Individually, students rate the activities on the chart.

Students rank the activities from 1 (the activity they like best) to 12 (the activity they like least).

Arrange students into small groups to discuss and compare their opinions. The group discusses options and agrees on a plan for the weekend—two activities for Saturday, two activities for Sunday, and what time of day they will meet.

Answers:

This is a personalization activity with no specific answers.

Optional Activity 6.2

Finding a Roommate, *page 125*

Preparation: Make one copy of Optional Activity 6.2 for each student.

Procedure: Distribute one copy of the handout to each student and explain the scenario.

Individually, students complete the Personal Information Form. After students have finished, arrange students into groups of four. Collect the Personal Information Forms and switch them with a different group, so that groups are now working with another groups' profiles.

Groups read each classmate's profile and discuss which student profile below (1-5) is best suited to each classmate.

Note: Student profiles 1–5 are numbered rather than named so they can be male or female as required.

Once groups have agreed on a match, they write the student number (1-5) on their classmate's Personal Information Form and groups return the forms to the original group. Students should be ready to explain their decision if a classmate complains!

Optional Activity 7.1

I always brush my teeth. *page 126*

Preparation: Bring dice (one for each group of 4–6 students) and counters (one for each student). Make one copy of Optional Activity 7.1 for each group.

Procedure: Arrange students into groups of 4–6 students. Distribute handouts, dice, and counters to each group. Students sit around a table to play this game. Game play and rules are printed at the top of each handout.

Students take turns, read the square to the group, and give an answer. Students miss a turn when they cannot complete an answer or repeat an answer previously given.

Someone from the group can ask a personal question when the player lands on **Personal Question**. Players can avoid answering by saying why they won't answer, for example, *Oh, that's too personal.*

Landing on **Free Turn** means players can throw again and move forward immediately.

Answers:

This is a personalization board game with no specific answers.

Optional Activity 7.2

Personality Quiz, *page 127*

Preparation: Make one copy of Optional Activity 7.2 for each student.

Procedure: Arrange students into small groups. Distribute one copy of the handout to each student.

Students discuss the questions.

Individually, students read and rate the statements.

Students find the description of their personality.

Students discuss the questions with a partner.

Answers:

This is a personalization activity with no specific answers.

NOTE: The statements and descriptions used in this activity are not scientifically proven. They are loosely based on introvert/extrovert/Type A/Type B personality types.

Optional Activity 8.1

Odd Man Out, *page 128*

Preparation: Make one copy of Optional Activity 8.1 for each student.

Procedure: Arrange students into small groups. Distribute one copy of the handout to each student.

In pairs, students read the sets of words and underline the three odd words in each set.

Students read each word list again and find the matching category name from the list.

Students review the odd words from the lists in Part 1 and choose six words that can make a new category.

Answers:

Part 1

Example   1. salad, fried, England

2. coffee, banana, pizza
3. dessert, fish, mushroom
4. bread, olive, Thai
5. sushi, carrot, egg
6. apple, seafood, beef curry

Part 2

1. nationalities
2. meat
3. drinks
4. desserts
5. sweets
6. dairy

Part 3

Extra Category

Name: fruits and vegetables

Words: salad, banana, mushroom, olive, carrot, apple

Optional Activity 8.2

Memory Cards, *page 129*

Preparation: Make one copy of Optional Activity 8.2 for every 5-6 students in class. Cut the copies into game play sheets, and individual memory cards.

Procedure: Arrange students into groups of 5-6. Distribute one copy of the game play sheet, and one set of memory cards to each group.

Students sit around a table. The cards are placed face down in the center of the table.

A player turns over two cards, reads them aloud to the group, and then tries to make a connection between the two cards. For example, if two cards read *lunch* and *sandwich*, the student could say, *We eat sandwiches for lunch.*

If the group agrees that there is a connection, the student keeps the cards and tries again.

If the group does not agree there is a connection, the cards are turned face down again, and another student takes a turn.

A player/group may appeal to the teacher for a final decision on a connection. The game ends when all cards have been collected or when the time limit has expired.

Answers:

This is an open association activity with no specific answers. If students can form associations and defend them to the group/teacher, then the answer is correct.

Optional Activity 9.1

Who am I? *page 130*

Preparation: Make one copy of Optional Activity 9.1 for every 4-5 students in class. Cut the sheet into the word box, and the cards.

Procedure: Arrange students into groups of 4-5. Distribute one list of professions to each group.

Ask groups to use the student book to write a list of qualities for each profession in the list—qualities they would expect to find and qualities they would not like to see in each profession. You can let the students use their lists during the game or challenge them by collecting the lists before they play.

Place the stack of cards face down on the table between the players.

A student volunteers to be the first player, takes a card from the top of the pile, and asks "Who am I?"

The group has 60 seconds to ask Yes/No questions about the qualities of the profession on the card. Information questions are not permitted.

The student may give *small* hints about the qualities if the group is having trouble guessing, but they MUST NOT say what the profession is or give obvious clues.

Members of the group must guess the role at the end of the 60-second time limit. They should not say the profession earlier, even if they think they know. Instead, they should ask more questions to confirm their guess.

When the profession has been identified, another student takes a new card, and the game continues until all students have picked a card.

Answers:

This is an open, collaborative activity with no specific answers.

Additional practice: Students work in pairs or small groups to create profiles of other professions and play the game again.

Optional Activity 9.2

The Candidates, *page 131*

Preparation: Make one copy of Optional Activity 9.2 for each student.

Procedure: Arrange students into groups of three. Distribute one copy of the handout to each student.

Students read the job openings to each other and then use the candidate profiles to select the best candidate(s) for each job. They should note down the reasons why they selected the candidates for each opening and why they rejected others.

Arrange students into new pairs and have them compare and discuss their choices for the job openings.

Answers:

This is a discussion activity with no correct/specific answers.

Additional Practice:

Pair discussion.

1. Would you apply for any of these job openings? Why? Why not?

2. Which job opening would best suit you?

3. Have you ever had a summer job?

Optional Activity 10.1

Find someone who... *page 132*

Preparation: Make one copy of Optional Activity 10.1 for each student.

Procedure: Arrange students into pairs. Distribute one copy of the handout to each student.

Students read through the cues, discuss, and agree on how to ask the questions. Remind them to be careful of the negative (never) statement in the list!

Students interview individual classmates until they find someone who can say that a piece of information is true for them. The student writes the person's name next to the cue on the list. The student continues to interview this person to find out and write down more specific information. Students should try to get as many names and additional details on their sheet as possible.

Answers:

This is an interview activity with no correct/specific answers.

Additional Practice: Students sit in small groups and share/discuss the information they discovered during the interviews.

Optional Activity 10.2

Find the Differences, *page 133*

Preparation: Make one copy of Optional Activity 10.2, which consists of *Student A* and *Student B*, for each pair of students. Cut the copies to separate the two parts.

Procedure: Arrange students into pairs. Distribute *Student A* to one student and *Student B* to the other.

Ask the class, *Where's the City Swimming Complex?* and *Can you tell me where to find the train station?*

Students work together to ask and answer questions about their town maps. Without looking at each other's maps, the partners must discover the (four) differences between their maps.

Answers:

These landmarks are the same:

1. Mullaley Mall is on Locke Lane, between Wiley Way and River Road.

2. The City Swimming Complex is on Streit Street, between River Road and Avalon Avenue.

3. Civic Park is on the corner of Streit Street and River Road, across from the City Swimming Complex.

4. The Train Station is on the corner of Locke Lane and Octopus Place.

5. Pineapple Plaza is between Locke Lane and Streit Street, in front of the Train Station.

The differences are:

1. In A, Green's Gym is between Wiley Way and River Road, between Civic Park and Mullaley Mall. In B, Green's Gym is between River Road and Pineapple Plaza, in front of the City Swimming Complex.

2. In A, the Post Office is between River Road and Pineapple Plaza, in front of the City Swimming Complex. In B, the Post Office is between Wiley Way and River Road, between Civic Park and Mullaley Mall.

3. In A, the bank is on Avalon Avenue, across from the City Swimming Complex. There is no bank in B.

4. In A, there is no coffee shop. In B, the coffee shop is on Locke Lane, between Mullaley Mall and the Train Station.

Optional Activity 11.1

Neither a lender nor a borrower be. *page 134*

Preparation: Make one copy of Optional Activity 11.1 for each student.

Procedure: Arrange students into small groups. Distribute one copy of the handout to each student.

Students read through the list of items in their small groups and check which items they own. More information about each item could be asked for and shared if time permits, for example, *What kind of car do you have?*

Students tell each other which items they would lend to the people in the list.

Students discuss general questions on the topic of lending and borrowing items.

Answers:

This is a personalization activity with no correct/specific answers.

Optional Activity 11.2

Hand it over! *page 135*

Preparation: Make two copies of Optional Activity 11.2 for each group of 5-6 players. Cut both copies of the activity into game play and a double set of individual playing cards. Shuffle the double sets before giving them to each group.

Procedure: Arrange students into groups of 5-6 around a table. Place the double set of cards in a stack, face down on the table. Each player takes three cards from the top of the stack but does not show them to the group.

Players take turns around the table, asking someone in the group for a matching card. The objective is for players to gather as many pairs of cards as possible.

For example, a student takes a card which reads *toothpaste*, looks at another player and asks, *Can you lend me your toothpaste?*

If that person has the card, they must hand it over. Students display pairs of cards on the table in front of them.

If a student asks the wrong person, he/she takes another card from the stack. The next player takes a turn.

The game ends when all the cards are in pairs on the table, or when the time limit expires.

Such a strange language! *page 136*

Preparation: Make one copy of Optional Activity 12.1, which consists of three parts, for each pair of students. Cut the copies into three.

Procedure: Arrange students into pairs. Distribute the silent letter activity handout to each pair.

In pairs, students read the words aloud and find the odd word in each line. The answer is in the pronunciation. Elicit the answers/model the pronunciation of each set of words to help students recognize the concept of silent letters in spoken English.

Students discuss other words they know with silent letters (for example, *one, lamb, two*). Students share these words with the class.

Distribute *Student A* and *Student B* cards to each pair. Ask students not to show their cards to their partner.

Student A starts reading the text to Student B who writes the missing words in the text. When A has a space, B continues reading, and A writes the missing words in his/her text. Students continue until both texts are completed. Students should compare their texts to confirm their answers from the dictation.

Answers:

Part 1

1. D. though
2. B. debit card
3. C. keep

Part 2

Did you ever wonder why English pronunciation is so strange? When the printing press arrived in England in the middle of the seventeenth century, spelling was based on the way people pronounced the words. Silent letters in words we use today, such as the K in knee or the L in would, were still pronounced in seventeenth century England. Spelling stayed the same but pronunciation continued to change, especially as English speakers began to settle in new places like North America, Australia, India, and South Africa.

Planning for the Future, *page 137*

Preparation: Make one copy of Optional Activity 12.2 for each student.

Procedure: Distribute one copy of the handout to each student. Elicit some things students plan to do in the future—in five years and in 15 years.

Ask students to complete the chart with personal goals they would like to achieve in the next five years and the next 15 years for each area of their life.

Arrange students into pairs. Students share and discuss their five-year goals only. Ask the class: *Are your goals similar or different from your partner's? What plans do you have to work towards your goals?*

In large groups or as a class, ask students to imagine that you are all now 15 years older and that everyone is attending a class reunion. Ask students to introduce themselves to each other and start a conversation. Students should try to discuss the 15-year goals they set, and whether they reached them. Students should have conversations with at least three other students. The activity ends when the time limit is up.

Part 1   Many names in English have a proper form (long form) and a nickname (short form).
For example, if your name is Robert, people can also call you Bob. Work with a partner and
match the proper names with the correct nicknames.

Proper name	Nickname
1. Robert ___	A. Jim
2. William ___	B. Kate
3. Patricia ___	C. Bob
4. Henry ___	D. Tony
5. Katherine ___	E. Pat
6. Edward ___	F. Beth
7. Christina ___	G. Ted
8. James ___	H. Bill
9. Richard ___	I. Chris
10. Elizabeth ___	J. Hank
11. Anthony ___	K. Dick

Part 2   Work with a partner. Choose a proper name from the list and practice the
conversation below.

Example

A: *Is your name* <u>Robert</u>?

B: *Yes, it is. You can call me* <u>Bob</u>.

Part 3   Work in small groups and discuss these questions.

1. What are three popular names for girls in your country?
2. What are three popular names for boys in your country?
3. Do people use nicknames in your country?
4. Can you think of any famous English-speaking people with nicknames? Who?
5. Do you have a nickname? Who uses it? Do you like it? How did you get it?

Part 1 Work in groups of three. Use the word grid to help you complete the conversation.

are	1. How	Ben.	that	girl?	4. She's
you	thanks	5. She's	3. Who's	neighbor	my
2. Fine	today?	really	Tina.	is	my
6. Do	cute.	meet	8. this	classmate	you.
you	to	her?	do.	Ben.	meet
want	7. I	sure	9. It's	nice	to

Example   1. Ben: Hi, Yang. *How are you today?*

2. **Yang:** _____. _____, _____. How are you?

3. **Ben:** Fine. _____ _____ _____?

4. **Yang:** _____ _____ _____, _____.

5. **Ben:** _____ _____ _____.

6. **Yang:** _____ _____ _____ _____ _____ _____?

7. **Ben:** _____ _____ _____.

8. **Yang:** Tina, _____ _____ _____ _____, _____.

9. **Tina:** Hi, Ben. _____ _____ _____ _____ you.

10. **Ben:** *(What do you think Ben says?)* _____.

Part 2 Continue the conversation in your group.

Optional Activity 1.2 **115**

Part 1 Work with a partner. Rearrange the letters in the following words to spell different clothing items and accessories. Example: HTRSOS = <u>shorts</u>

1. ARSETWE   _____
2. USIT   _____
3. CSOSK   _____
4. NGRIS   _____
5. PCEHENLOL   _____ _____
6. ACP   _____

7. HTSTRI   ____-_____
8. USASLSENSG   _____
9. LABLURME   _____
10. CWTAH   _____
11. NAESSEKR   _____

Part 2 Read the clues. Write the correct words from Part 1 on the lines.

1. Use it in the rain   __ __ __ __ __ __ __
2. Wear it on your head   __ __ __
3. Keeps the time   __ __ __ __ __
4. Call your friends with this   __ __ __ __ __ __ __ __ __
5. Wear it with jeans or shorts   __-__ __ __ __ __
6. Wear them for running   __ __ __ __ __ __ __ __
7. Protects your eyes   __ __ __ __ __ __ __ __
8. Keep your feet warm   __ __ __ __ __
9. Wear it for business   __ __ __ __
10. Wear them on your fingers   __ __ __ __ __
11. Keeps you warm   __ __ __ __ __ __ __

Part 3 Look at the words you wrote in the puzzle. Can you find the mystery word? Write it in the spaces below.

What's something you wear at the beach?   __ __ __ __ __ __ __ __ __ __

Optional Activity 2.2: Picture Dictation

Part 1   Work in pairs. Write the name of the items below.

1. _____   2. _____   3. _____   4. _____

5. _____   6. _____   7. _____   8. _____

Part 2   Individually, choose six items and draw them in the picture below.

Part 3   Describe your picture and where the six items are to your partner. Your partner will draw them in his/her picture. Compare your pictures. Are they the same?

Part 4   Listen to your partner describe his/her picture. Draw items in the picture below. Compare your pictures. Are they the same?

Optional Activity 2.2 **117**

Student X
Name: George Yip
Age: _____   Birthday: _____
Height: _____   Weight: _____
Nationality: _____
Interests: _____ & _____

Student Y
Name: Eva King
Age: _____   Birthday: _____
Height: _____   Weight: _____
Nationality: _____
Interests: _____ & _____

Student X
Name: _____
Age: 32   Birthday: March 23rd
Height: _____   Weight: _____
Nationality: _____
Interests: _____ & _____

Student Y
Name: _____
Age: 24   Birthday: October 7th
Height: _____   Weight: _____
Nationality: _____
Interests: _____ & _____

Student X
Name: _____
Age: _____   Birthday: _____
Height: 180 cm   Weight: 80 kg
Nationality: _____
Interests: _____ & _____

Student Y
Name: _____
Age: _____   Birthday: _____
Height: 160 cm   Weight: 58 kg
Nationality: _____
Interests: _____ & _____

Student X
Name: _____
Age: _____   Birthday: _____
Height: _____   Weight: _____
Nationality: American
Interests: _____ & _____

Student Y
Name: _____
Age: _____   Birthday: _____
Height: _____   Weight: _____
Nationality: German
Interests: _____ & _____

Student X
Name: _____
Age: _____   Birthday: _____
Height: _____   Weight: _____
Nationality: _____
Interests: Baseball & Travel

Student Y
Name: _____
Age: _____   Birthday: _____
Height: _____   Weight: _____
Nationality: _____
Interests: Tennis & Fashion

Part 1   Work in groups. Fill in the blanks with the matching family term.

Male	**Female**
grandfather	grandmother
father	_____
_____	aunt
brother	_____
_____	niece
boyfriend	_____

Part 2   Imagine that your group is one family. Discuss the following questions and describe the members of your family. Use the family/relationship words to help you.

1. What is your family name?
2. What are the names of the people in your family? Do they have nicknames?
3. How are the members in your group related?
   For example: *Who is the mother, the father…?*
4. How old is each person?
5. What does each person do?
6. List two or more interests each person has.

Use the space below to note the basic information about your new family.

	Person 1	Person 2	Person 3	Person 4	Person 5
Name:	_____	_____	_____	_____	_____
Family role:	_____	_____	_____	_____	_____
Age:	_____	_____	_____	_____	_____
Occupation:	_____	_____	_____	_____	_____
Interests:	_____	_____	_____	_____	_____

Part 3   Present your new family to the class. Take turns answering questions that your classmates ask about your new family.

Part 1   Look at the picture at the bottom of the page for one minute. Then fold the page and hide the picture.

Part 2   Answer these questions about the picture.

Score

1. Who is the first person in line? _____   _____
2. Who is standing next to the older man? _____   _____
3. What is the little girl doing? _____   _____
4. What is in the older man's hand? _____   _____
5. What is the teenage boy wearing? _____   _____
6. Who is wearing sandals? _____   _____
7. What does the woman's hair look like? _____   _____
8. What is the older man looking at? _____   _____
9. Who is the tallest person? _____   _____
10. Who has the backpack? _____   _____
11. What is on the little girl's shirt? _____   _____
12. Who is the last person in line? _____   _____

Part 3   Compare your answers with your partner.

Part 4   Count your correct answers. Check your score on the chart and see how observant you are.

Scores

11–12   Fantastic memory! You would be a star witness.

8–10   Good memory. You can often help people find misplaced objects.

6–7   OK memory. You get lost sometimes but not for long.

5 or less Keep trying! Don't forget to look at things carefully.

Student A

1. Work with a partner. Complete the information about the items you must sell.

2. You must sell your items and buy four items. Ask a classmate what items they are selling and decide if you want to buy them. When you buy an item fill the information in.

SELL

Price _____	_____	_____	_____
Color _____	_____	_____	_____
Qualities _____	_____	_____	_____

BUY

Man's watch	Roller blades	T-shirt	Sofa
Price _____	_____	_____	_____
Color _____	_____	_____	_____
Qualities _____	_____	_____	_____

✂ -

Student B

1. Work with a partner. Complete the information about the items you must sell.

2. You must sell your items and buy four items. Ask a classmate what items they are selling and decide if you want to buy them. When you buy an item fill the information in.

SELL

Price _____	_____	_____	_____
Color _____	_____	_____	_____
Qualities _____	_____	_____	_____

BUY

Necklace and Earrings	Arm chair	Girl's bike	Sweater
Price _____	_____	_____	_____
Color _____	_____	_____	_____
Qualities _____	_____	_____	_____

Student A Work in pairs. Ask questions to complete the missing information about Ben's day.

You ask your partner: *How old is Ben?*   Your partner answers: *He is 34 years old.*
Your partner asks: *Where does he live?*   You answer: *He lives in Chicago.*

Ben is (Ex.) <u>34</u>-years-old. He lives in <u>**Chicago**</u> and is married to (1) _____ They have two children, a son, (2) _____ who is (3) _____-years-old and a daughter, May, who is five-years-old. Ben is a (4) _____. He likes his job very much, but he has an unusual daily routine. Ben gets up at 3 A.M. He leaves home at (5) _____ and walks to the bakery. He has breakfast at the bakery at 3:45 A.M. and starts baking for the day at (6) _____. The bakery opens at 7 A.M. It is very busy. Around (7) _____, Ben has lunch and at 9 A.M., he cleans the kitchen and starts preparing for the next day. He finishes work at (8) _____ and gets home at 2 P.M. He eats a big dinner with his wife at (9) _____ and they talk about the day. At 3 P.M., he leaves home to meet Ty and May at their school, and they all walk home together. Ben plays with his children until the children's dinner time at (10) _____. Ben likes to sit with them and have a cup of tea. At 6 P.M. he watches the news on TV. After the news, he kisses his wife and children good night and he goes to bed at 8:15 P.M.

✂ -

Student B Work in pairs. Ask questions to complete the missing information about Ben's day.

Your partner asks: *How old is Ben?*   You answer: *He is 34 years old.*
You ask your partner: *Where does he live?*   Your partner answers *He lives in Chicago.*

Ben is <u>34</u>-years-old. He lives in (Ex.) <u>**Chicago**</u> and is married to Sung-Yi. They have (1) _____ children, a son, Ty, who is seven-years-old and a daughter, (2) _____, who is (3) _____-years-old. Ben is a baker. He likes his job very much, but he has an unusual daily routine. Ben gets up at (4) _____. He leaves home at 3:25 A.M. and walks to the bakery. He has breakfast at the bakery at (5) _____ and starts baking for the day at 4 A.M. The bakery opens at (6) _____. It is very busy. Around 8:15 A.M., Ben has lunch and at (7) _____, he cleans the kitchen and starts preparing for the next day. He finishes work at 1:30 P.M. and gets home at (8) _____. He eats a big dinner with his wife at 2:10 P.M., and they talk about the day. At (9) _____, he leaves home to meet Ty and May at their school, and they all walk home together. Ben plays with his children until the children's dinner time at 5 P.M. Ben likes to sit with them and have a cup of tea. At (10) _____ he watches the news on TV. After the news, he kisses his wife and children good night, and he goes to bed at 8:15 P.M.

Student A

Part 1   Plan a day trip to Montreal. Work with your partner to complete the missing information.

Tourist Information–Montreal, Canada

CULTURAL

Museum of Fine Arts	Tues.-Sun., 11 A.M.-5 P.M., Wed. 5-9 P.M. (half price) Closed Mon.	*Admission $*_____
World Weather Museum	October-May: _____	*Admission $6.50*
Notre Dame Cathedral	Daily 8 A.M.-4 P.M.	Free tours

RECREATION

Indoor Ice skating	_____, Fri. & Sat. 11:30 A.M.–7 P.M., Fri. & Sat. 7 P.M.–midnight (16 years and older)	*Admission $5.00*
Boating on the Rapids	_____ Departs every 2 hours.	Tickets $15.00
Casino	Open 24 hours. (18 years and older)	_____ *Admission*

ENTERTAINMENT

Arts Palace	*Lion King:* Daily (except Tues.), 8 P.M.; Wed. & Sat. 2 P.M.	*Tickets $*_____
IMAX Cinema	*Robots:* Daily____, ____, ____. Extra show Fri. 11 P.M.	*Tickets $ 12.00*
Botanical Gardens	_____ May-October, 9 A.M.-6 P.M. daily. (Free tours at 10 A.M. & 1 P.M.)	*Admission $6.00*

Part 2   Work with your partner and use the completed sheet to decide what to see and do on your day trip. You have 13 hours in Montreal. Your bus arrives at 9 A.M. and leaves at 10 P.M. You have a budget of $75.00 for the day.

✂ --

Student B

Part 1   Plan a day trip to Montreal. Work with your partner to complete the missing information.

Tourist Information–Montreal, Canada

CULTURAL

Museum of Fine Arts	_____, Wed. 5-9 P.M. (half price) Closed Mon.	*Admission $10.00*
World Weather Museum	October–May: Mon., Wed., Thurs., Fri., 12-5 P.M.	*Admission $*_____
Notre Dame Cathedral	_____	Free tours

RECREATION

Indoor Ice skating	Sun.-Thurs., 11:30 A.M.-9 P.M. _____ Fri. & Sat., 7 P.M.–midnight (16 years and older)	*Admission $*_____
Boating on the Rapids	May 1–October 15: Daily 10 A.M.–6 P.M. Departs every 2 hours.	*Tickets $*_____
Casino	_____. (18 years and older)	*Free Admission*

ENTERTAINMENT

Arts Palace	*Lion King:* _____; Wed. & Sat. 2 P.M.	*Tickets $25.00-$75.00*
IMAX Cinema	*Robots:* Daily 2:30, 4:45, 7:00. Extra show Fri. 11 P.M.	*Tickets $*_____
Botanical Gardens	November-May: Tues.-Sun. 9 A.M.–5 P.M. May-October: 9 A.M.–6 P.M. daily. (Free tours at _____ & _____)	*Admission $6.00*

Part 2   Work with your partner and use the completed sheet to decide what to see and do on your day trip. You have 13 hours in Montreal. Your bus arrives at 9 A.M. and leaves at 10 P.M. You have a budget of $75.00 for the day.

Part 1   What do you like to do on the weekends? Mark your opinion of the activities on the chart.

Activity	Like a lot	Good	OK	Don't like	Rank
Sleep					
Go to a rock concert					
Go to the library/Study					
Go shopping for clothes					
Watch a video at home					
Go dancing all night					
See an English movie					
Play a team sport					
Go to a foreign restaurant					
Go to a museum					
Go to the gym					
Your idea:					

Part 2   Rank the activities in order of preference from 1-12 (1 = favorite, 12 = least favorite). Then in small groups compare and discuss your opinions about the different activities.

Part 3   Make weekend plans with the people in your group. Discuss the options and agree on two activities for Saturday and two activities for Sunday. Finally, decide what time you will meet.

Useful Expressions

How do you feel about…?	I think it's great/good/OK/awful.
How do you like…?	I like it a lot./I don't like it.
Which day do you want to…?	How about Saturday/Sunday?
When is a good time to…?	Saturday…morning/afternoon/night at + time.

Part 1 For one month this summer, you will study English at a summer school in Scotland. Complete the form with your own information.

Haggis Language School

Personal Information Form

Name: _____ Age: _____ City/Country: _____

Current study/work: _____ Languages spoken: _____

Countries/Cities visited: _____

Interests (sports, music, movies, games, hobbies, etc.):

_____

_____

Write 3 qualities to describe yourself:

1. _____ 2. _____ 3. _____

Part 2 Work in groups. Switch papers with another group. Read the information above. Then read the student profiles below. Decide which student would be the best roommate for the person above. Why?

Student 1   Moscow, Russia
Age: 24
Study: Art History
Languages: Russian, French
Music: Classical, Jazz
Sports: Karate, Tai Chi
Movies: Historical, Martial Arts
Hobbies: Painting, Chess
Travel: Poland, Paris, Tokyo
Qualities: serious, quiet, relaxed

Student 2   Lisbon, Portugal
Age: 19
Study: Mechanical Engineering
Languages: Portuguese, Spanish
Music: Pop, Dance
Sports: Soccer, Cycling
Movies: Action, Comedy
Hobbies: Cooking
Travel: Brazil, New York, Boston
Qualities: outgoing, reliable, talkative

Student 3   Cairo, Egypt
Age: 22
Study: Computer Science
Languages: Arabic
Music: Techno, Punk
Sports: Golf, Swimming
Movies: Romance, Horror
Hobbies: Video games, Scuba diving
Travel: South Africa, Chile
Qualities: patient, shy, smart

Student 4   Puebla, Mexico
Age: 25
Job: Tennis instructor
Languages: Spanish, German
Music: Rock, Blues
Sports: Tennis, Squash
Movies: All except horror
Hobbies: Reading, Hiking
Travel: Caribbean, Germany
Qualities: curious, messy, calm

Student 5   Quebec City, Canada
Age: 20
Study: Business
Languages: French, some Italian
Music: All kinds
Sports: Skiing, Basketball
Movies: Dramas, Science fiction
Hobbies: Photography
Travel: Vancouver, Thailand
Qualities: fun, entertaining, late

How to play:

- Take turns rolling the die and moving your counter forward.

- Read your square aloud to the group and give your answer.

- If you cannot complete the answer, you must miss a turn.

- If a player repeats a previous answer to the same question, they automatically miss a turn.

- **Personal Question** means your group can ask you a personal question. You can choose not to answer, but you must say why you won't answer.

- **Free Turn** means you can throw again immediately.

- The winner is the player who successfully answers the final clue first.

To play this game, you need a group of 4-6 players, a die, and a counter for each player.

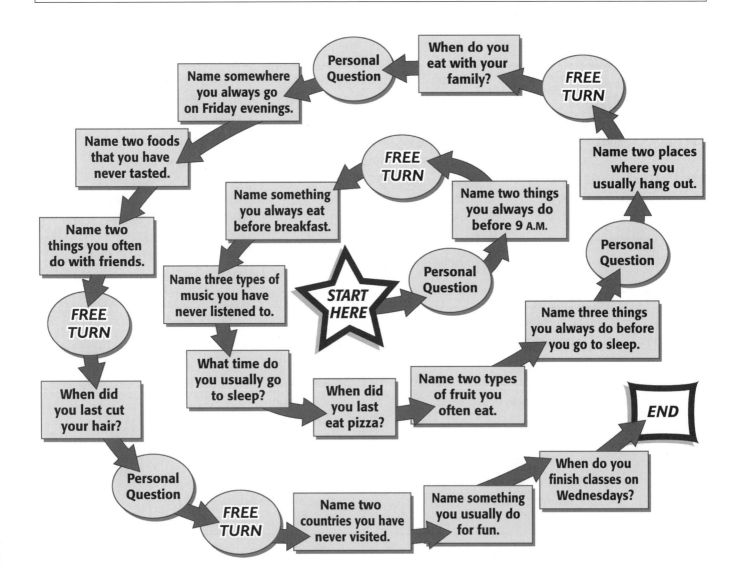

Part 1 Work in small groups and discuss these questions.

1. What magazines do you read?
2. Do you always buy them?
3. Do you like answering magazine quizzes?
4. What can they tell you?

Part 2 Answer these questions by yourself.

	Always	Usually	Often	Sometimes	Never
1. I like meeting new people.					
2. I have strong opinions.					
3. I feel nervous in new situations.					
4. I like to organize people.					
5. I find it hard to start conversations.					
6. I like who I am.					
7. I enjoy new situations.					
8. I don't like wasting time.					
9. I like trying new things.					
10. I worry a lot.					
11. I have a lot of energy.					

Part 3 Find your description below.

A) *You answered "Always" or "Usually" for questions 2, 4, 8, and 10, and "Never" for questions 3 and 5.*

You are a natural leader and you set yourself goals and work hard to achieve them. You are very active, but you often feel stressed and tired. You should try to set fewer goals and let other people make the decisions sometimes.

B) *You answered "Always" or "Usually" for questions 2, 3, 5, and 10, and "Never" for questions 4, 7, and 9.*

You are quiet and like to let other people do the talking and take the lead. You are thoughtful and sensitive, and people respect your opinions when you share them. You should try new things and try to share how you feel more often.

C) *You answered "Always" or "Usually" for questions 1, 7, 9, and 11, and "Never" for questions 3 and 5.*

You enjoy meeting new people and you make friends easily. You love to try new things, and people love being around you. You should try to listen to other people more often and think more before you speak.

Part 4 Discuss the questions below with a partner.

1. What does the quiz say about your personality?
2. Does it describe you correctly?
3. Have you ever taken a quiz like this before? Tell your partner about the experience.

Optional Activity 7.2 **127**

Part 1 Work with a partner. Read each set of words. Underline the three words that don't belong in each set.

Example	1. <u>salad</u>	Chinese	Mexican	<u>fried</u>	Korean	Indian	<u>England</u>	Canadian
2. beef	sausage	coffee	lamb	banana	bacon		pizza	chicken
3. juice	dessert	milk	soda	tea	fish		soy milk	mushroom
4. bread	cake	apple pie	olive	cookie	Thai		ice cream	brownie
5. sushi	raisin	carrot	soda	egg	juice		cookie	ice cream sundae
6. milk	cheese	milkshake	apple	seafood	sour cream		yogurt	beef curry

Part 2 Read each set of words above again. Write the matching category name below.

    dairy   drinks   desserts   sweets   meat   nationalities

1. _____

2. _____

3. _____

4. _____

5. _____

6. _____

Part 3 Can you make a new category with six odd words from the lists?

    Category Name: _____

    Words: 1. <u>salad</u>   2. _____   3. _____

                4. _____   5. _____   6. _____

How to play:

- Sit around a table so everyone can see the cards.

- Place all the cards face down in the center of the table.

- A player turns over two cards, reads them aloud to the group, and then tries to make a connection between the two cards. For example, if your two cards read *lunch* and *sandwich*, you could say: *We eat sandwiches for lunch.*

- If the group agrees that there is a connection, the player keeps the cards and tries again.

- If the group does not agree there is a connection, the cards are turned face down again, and another player takes a turn.

To play this game you need a group of 5–6 players and a set of memory cards.

✂ -

sweet	meal	water	iced tea	toast
cold	breakfast	tea	seafood	fish
hot	lunch	coffee	salad	cereal
light	dinner	rice	fruit	sandwich
small	snack	noodles	banana	fast food
spicy	curry	yellow	egg	hamburger

Optional Activity 9.1: Who am I?

sailor	chef	bank teller	police officer
artist	dentist	teacher	actor
driving instructor	nurse	airline pilot	window cleaner

© 2006 Oxford University Press. Permission granted to photocopy for classroom use.

Part 1   Work in small groups, and read the job openings below. Then select the best candidates for each job. Write the reasons why you selected the candidates for each job.

Job Openings

WooHoo Winter Escapes Inc.: Resort Hosts

Looking for three young adults to spend two months living and working at an international winter holiday resort. Successful candidates will:

- speak at least two languages.
- enjoy meeting new people.
- love adventure.
- be good at winter sports.

BaDaBooom Music Co.: Pop Stars

Auditioning young musicians who want to be members of the BigBopBand. This is the opportunity of a lifetime if you are outgoing, creative, and flexible. To be selected as a member you must:

- play a musical instrument.
- work well with other people.
- be able to dance.
- sing in tune.

Camp Capboom: Camp Counselors

We are looking for 15 responsible individuals to spend the summer with us at Camp Capboom. Spend the summer swimming in the lake and hiking in the mountains with groups of children and teenagers. You must:

- like working with people.
- be adventurous and ready to try anything.
- be a good listener.
- be caring and understanding.

The Candidates

Name: JILL	Name: JUANITA
Sex: Female Age: 23	Sex: Female Age: 54
Height: 170 cm	Height: 160 cm
Languages: Korean/English	Languages: Spanish/English
Sports: tennis/canoeing/swimming	Sports: ice skating/snowboarding/skiing
Likes: exercising/traveling	Likes: singing/dancing
Name: VLAD	Name: SEO WOO
Sex: Male Age: 16	Sex: Male Age: 25
Height: 175 cm	Height: 185 cm
Languages: Russian	Languages: Korean/English/French
Sports: surfing/skiing/hiking	Sports: baseball/basketball/volleyball
Likes: computer games/reading	Likes: meeting friends/playing the guitar

Part 2   Work with a new partner and discuss the choices you made for each job opening.

Part 1 Work with a partner. Read through the cues below. Discuss and agree on how to ask the questions. Be careful of the negative statement in the list!

Part 2 Interview classmates until you find someone who the information is true for. Write that person's name below, then interview him/her to get more information about his/her answer. Try to get as many names and details as possible.

Names	Find someone who...	Details
_____	is wearing white socks.	_____
_____	always travels on public transportation.	_____
_____	can give directions to the nearest bus stop.	_____
_____	bought a new pair of sunglasses last year.	_____
_____	often rides a bicycle to class.	_____
_____	never buys shoes at a shoe store.	_____
_____	can remember the color of the school's front door.	_____
_____	gave someone the wrong directions by mistake.	_____
_____	uses the Internet everyday.	_____
_____	can tell you where to find the nearest movie theatre.	_____
_____	knows where to buy cheap books.	_____
_____	can name three important landmarks in your city.	_____

Student A

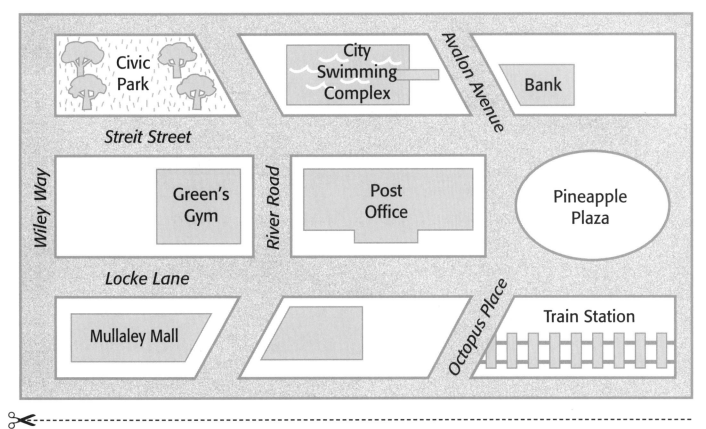

Student B

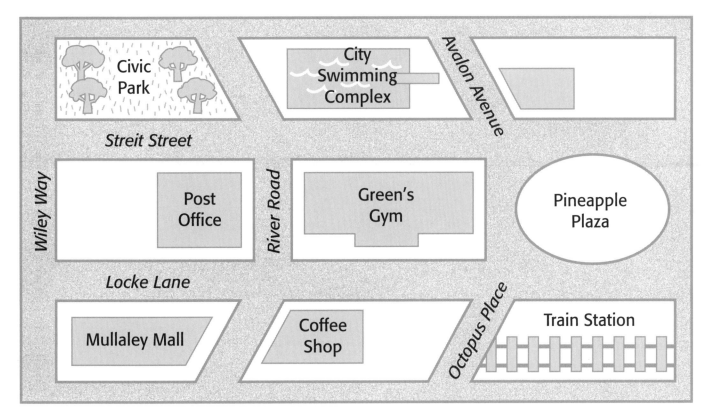

Part 1 Work in small groups. Read through the following items. Check (✓) the items you own.

watch ___	shampoo ___	bottle of water ___
hairbrush ___	toothbrush ___	text book ___
music CD ___	bathing suit ___	coffee cup ___
deodorant ___	pencil ___	winter coat ___
car ___	email address ___	eraser ___
credit card ___	jewelry ___	bath towel ___
class notes ___	running shoes ___	money ___
bicycle ___	shirt ___	passport ___

Part 2 Tell your group which items you would lend to the following people:

brother	classmate	stranger
neighbor	teacher	mother

Part 3 Discuss the questions below with your group.

1. What was the last thing you lent to someone?
2. What items do you sometimes borrow from other people? Do people always agree when you ask?
3. Do you often lend things to people when they ask? What are some ways can you say "No?"
4. Is there anything that you would never lend to anyone? Why?

How to play:

- Place all the cards face down in the center of the table.

- Each player takes three cards from the top of the stack but does not show them to the group.

- Take turns around the table. Ask someone in the group for a matching card. For example, you have one card which reads *toothpaste* . Look at another player and ask: *Can you lend me your toothpaste?* If that person has the card, they must hand it over to you. Put pairs on the table in front of you.

- If you asked the wrong person, take another card from the stack. The next player takes a turn.

USEFUL EXPRESSIONS:

Can you lend me your …?	Yes, I can./Sorry, I can't.
Could I borrow your …?	Sure./No, sorry.
Do you have (- / a / an) … I could borrow?	Here you are. or No, I don't.

To play this game you need a group of 5-6 students and two sets of cards.

✂ -

✂ -

email address	winter gloves	wedding ring	bar of soap	math textbook
summer house	hairbrush	MP3 player	toothbrush	earplugs
bottle of water	blue jeans	red shoes	bicycle	sandwich
desk lamp	boyfriend	motor bike	laptop computer	pet fish
bathing cap	bath towel	wristwatch	baseball cap	blank CD
money	teapot	English essay	deodorant	credit card

Optional Activity 12.1: Such a strange language!

Work with a partner. Read the words below aloud. Circle the word which does not belong in each line

1. A. laugh   B. cough   C. enough   D. though
2. A. comb   B. debit card   C. doubt   D. thumb
3. A. know   B. knee   C. keep   D. knight

What other words do you know that have silent letters? Share them with the class.

✂ -

Student A Read the words to your partner. He/She will write them down. When you have a space, listen and write the missing words that your partner reads.

Did you ever _____ _____ English _____ _____ _____ strange? _____ _____

printing press _____ _____ England in _____ _____ _____ _____ seventeenth

_____, spelling _____ _____ on the way _____ _____ the words. _____ letters in

words _____ _____ _____, such as _____ _____ in knee or the L _____

_____, were still pronounced _____ _____ century _____. _____ stayed the _____,

_____ pronunciation continued _____ _____, _____ as English _____ _____ to

settle in new _____ _____ _____ America, Australia, _____, _____ _____ Africa.

✂ -

Student B Listen and write the missing words your partner reads to you. When your partner has a space, read the words in your sentence so your partner can write them down.

_____ _____ _____ wonder why _____ pronunciation is so _____? When the

_____ _____ arrived in _____ _____ the middle of the _____ century, _____ was

based _____ _____ _____ people pronounced _____ _____. Silent _____

_____ _____ we use today, _____ _____ the K _____ _____ _____ _____

_____ in would, _____ _____ _____ in seventeenth _____ England. Spelling

_____ _____ same, but _____ _____ to change, especially _____ _____ speakers

began _____ _____ _____ _____ places like North _____, _____, India, and South

_____.

Part 1   Complete the chart with your personal goals.

	My 5-Year Goals	My 15-Year Goals
Employment and Career		
Partner and Family		
Language Abilities		
Study and Qualifications		
Lifestyle		

Part 2   Work with a partner and talk about your five-year goals.

Part 3   Imagine you are at a class reunion 15 years from now. Introduce yourself to a classmate and start a conversation. Discuss the goals you reached and talk about your life.